Study Guide

To Accompany

INTRODUCTION TO INTERNATIONAL ECONOMICS

Second Edition

Dominick Salvatore
Fordham University

Prepared By

Arthur Raymond
Muhlenberg College

WILEY

John Wiley & Sons, Inc.

To order books or for customer service call 1-800-CALL-WILEY (225-5945).

10 9 8 7 6 5 4 3 2 1

CONTENTS

To the Student

The purpose of this Study Guide is to provide the student with a relatively short chapter-by-chapter review of the second edition of Salvatore's *Introduction to International Economics*. Each chapter of this Study Guide is divided into the following parts:

- Chapter Outline
- Chapter Summary and Review
- Key Terms used in Chapter Summary and Review
- Multiple Choice Questions
- Problems and Discussion Questions

The Chapter Outline simply reproduces the outlines provided by Professor Salvatore, but is useful in providing a perspective on the contents of each chapter as you complete the study guide. Note that the Study Guide does not cover every topic listed in the Chapter Outline. The emphasis is on the most important underlying concepts necessary to understand the economics of international exchange. Although clearly important, historical accounts are not recounted in this Study Guide.

The Chapter Summary and Review section attempts to provide a brief development and description of the more important ideas in each chapter. Some of the summaries and reviews may also provide you with a different way of thinking about or approaching the material.

The Key Terms are provided as a quick check on your understanding of important ideas introduced in the Study Guide. The Key Terms listed in the Study Guide are terms used in the Chapter Summary and Review section of the Study Guide, so they may differ somewhat from the list provided by the textbook.

The Multiple Choice Questions and Problems and Discussion Questions are tests of your understanding of the material. If you can easily answer the questions in this Study Guide then you have a good understanding of the material in the text. It's better to answer the questions **before** consulting the answers provided at the end of the Study Guide. **Rather than reading a question and then quickly turning to the answer, commit your answers to paper before checking the answers provided at the back of the study guide.** It's clearly better to invest in an answer before reviewing the answers provided.

You will find that much of the analysis is conducted with diagrams and tables. The use of diagrams and tables are ways of organizing your thinking. The memory requirements for conducting much of the necessary analysis without aids like diagrams and tables are beyond most of us. Consequently, do not try to answer the questions by just looking at the diagrams and tables presented. **Put your pencil on the paper and draw your own diagrams and tables.**

Although there are probably many useful studying strategies, the following sequence for each chapter is suggested.

1. Read the chapter in the Salvatore textbook.

2. Review the Outline in the Study Guide. If any topic is unfamiliar return to the textbook and briefly review the topic.

3. Read the Summary and Review in the Study Guide.

4. Answer the problems in the Study Guide, committing your answers to paper. If necessary, refer to the textbook and the Summary and Review in the Study Guide to answer the questions.

5. Review the answers provided at the back of the Study Guide, comparing them to your answers.

6. Re-review the Outline in the Study Guide. If any topics are not familiar, return to the textbook and the Summary and Review.

7. Re-read the chapter in the Salvatore textbook.

Chapter 1
Introduction to the Global Economy

Chapter Outline

Chapter Summary and Review

International economic activity affects us all to varying degrees on a daily basis. The presence of international economic activity can be quite obvious as in the case of the use of imported goods by domestic consumers. Domestic consumers buy imported automobiles, wine, electronic goods, oil, etc. in order to take advantage of lower prices, variety, or better quality. Domestic corporations export insurance and accounting services, software, food, chemicals and medicine to other countries where such services are more expensive or non-existent.

In many cases the presence of international activity can be rather subtle. For example, many imports may not be used directly but are components of goods used by domestic consumers. Automobiles in the US, for example, are produced with both US and imported components.

International trade also affects purely domestic goods and services. Imports compete with domestic industries (**import-competing firms**), the result of which can often be better service, price, and variety for domestic consumers. Similarly, the effect of exports extends to other sectors of the economy. For example, export sectors often pay relatively high wages, drawing labor away from other sectors. The reduced supply of labor in the other sectors raises the wage rates in those other sectors.

International trade, the import and export of goods and services, is just one kind of international economic activity. For most countries, the movement of people across borders is also an important international economic activity. Approximately 45% of the US population growth between the years 2000 and 2003 was due to immigration.

Emigration and **immigration** affect the domestic price of goods, domestic wages, as well as social services and the character and diversity of many regions and communities.

Less apparent than international trade and the movement of people is the movement of financial capital from one nation to another – **foreign investment**. If interest rates and rates of return (adjusted for risk) differ across nations, then financial capital will flow out of nations with lower rates to nations with higher rates. This flow of financial capital will tend to equalize rates (adjusted for risk) across nations, so the interest rate paid on a home mortgage by a citizen in rural Idaho is determined by the worldwide market for capital, and is closely related to the interest rate paid on a penthouse by a citizen in Sao Paulo. The effect of the recent subprime mortgage crisis in the US was felt by many other nations.

The international flow of goods, people and financial capital also means a movement of currencies across borders. In order to import autos from Japan, an exchange of dollars for yen must take place. In order for an Italian pension fund to invest in the stock of IBM, an exchange of Euros for dollars must take place. Changes in these activities may cause a change in the **foreign exchange rate,** the rate at which one currency exchanges for another on the foreign exchange rate. The level of the foreign exchange rate is important to anyone involved with or affected by international economic activity. An **appreciation** of the US dollar (a more expensive dollar for those outside the US), for example, will hurt US exporters and help US importers and so will affect anyone associated directly or indirectly with US exports and US imports. Note that a more expensive US dollar for other nations is equivalent to cheaper foreign currency for US residents. Thus, an appreciation of the US dollar is equivalent to a **depreciation** of other currencies.

Within the past few years we have witnessed the formal establishment of an expanded international economy. In 2001 China, with more than one billion people, became part of the **World Trade Organization** (WTO). The WTO is currently made up of over 150 nations each of which have agreed to have the rules for trade decided at a world level rather than pursue isolation or restrict its trade negotiations to only a few trading partners. The WTO is an institution through which the nations of the world can meet and multilaterally agree to reduce the barriers to international exchange.

Alongside the WTO there are a number of regional international organizations that promote freer international activity among its members. Many nations are part of the WTO as well as these regional organizations. Some of the larger regional organizations include the **European Union** (EU), which in 2004 admitted ten countries that were formerly part of the Soviet bloc, the **North American Free Trade Agreement** (NAFTA) between Canada, Mexico and the US, and **Asia-Pacific Economic Cooperation** (APEC). Just as the EU is expanding, the **Free Trade of the Americas** (FTAA) has expanded to include 34 nations of the Americas. APEC, although a less formal organization than the WTO, EU and NAFTA, hopes to expand trade and investment among its 21 members that border the Pacific region. (The interested student can review the details of these international organizations with a web search.)

As is apparent from the recent debates about globalization, the effects of international economic activity are neither uniformly positive nor uniformly negative for each and every individual and constituency. Consumers may gain; some categories of labor may lose; others see trade as adversely affecting the environment. Most international economic activity produces gains to some groups and losses to others. Those who favor globalization see net gains from globalization, while the **anti-globalization movement** sees net losses from globalization. A major objective of international economics is to help understand how international activity, primarily trade, affects the distribution of income and the overall level of income within nations.

International economics is traditionally divided into international trade and **international finance**. The field of international trade focuses on the basis of trade between nations and the effect of that trade on the welfare of nations. International trade theory is surveyed in Parts I-III of the Salvatore text and this Study Guide. International finance includes the study of the **foreign-exchange market, the balance of payments** (the record of international inflows and outflows) and how international transactions affect GDP growth, unemployment, and inflation. Because a major emphasis of international finance is on macroeconomic variables like GDP growth, unemployment and inflation, international finance is often called **"open-economy macroeconomics."** International finance is considered in Parts IV-V of the Salvatore text and this Study Guide.

Key Terms used in Chapter Summary and Review
(The list below is not necessarily the same as the list provided by the Salvatore text.)

Anti-globalization Movement
Appreciation
Asia-Pacific Economic Cooperation
Balance of Payments
Depreciation
Emigration
European Union (EU)
Foreign Exchange Market
Foreign Exchange Rate

Foreign Investment
Free Trade of the Americas
Import-competing firms
International Trade
Immigration
International Finance
North American Free Trade Agreement
   (NAFTA)
Open Economy Macroeconomics
World Trade Organization (WTO)

Multiple Choice Questions

1. Imports will most likely
a) Increase the cost of living.
b) Increase competition to import-competing firms.
c) Compromise the quality of domestic goods.
d) Limit the variety of goods available to domestic consumers.

2. International trade refers to
a) Foreign investment.
b) Emigration and immigration.
c) The exchange of foreign currency.
d) Exports and Imports of goods and services

3. International organizations like the WTO, NAFA and APEC are
a) Part of the anti-globalization movement.
b) Opposed to increased international trade by nations.
c) In favor of freer trade between nations.
d) Exporters and importers.

4. According to Figure 1.2 of the text, world export growth from 1996-2006 has, on average, been
a) Greater than average world import growth.
b) Less than average world import growth.
c) Less than average world GDP growth.
d) Greater than world GDP growth.

5. According to Figure 1.3 exports of the US as a percentage of GDP in 2004:
a) Exceeds imports of the US as a percentage of GDP.
b) Is smaller than in 1970.
c) Has declined since 2000
d) was unchanged throughout the 1980s.

Problems and Discussion Questions

1. Suppose the US implements a trade policy that produces an increase in imports.
a) What special-interest groups in the US will most likely gain from the increased imports?

b) What special-interest groups in the US will most likely lose from the increased imports? (Special interest groups include consumers; various industries; e.g. the domestic auto and computer industries; workers in different industries, e.g. steel workers and textile workers; and groups representing social causes like environmentalists and those supporting reform of working conditions.)

2. a) How would each individual's standard of living be affected if each individual decided to be completely self-reliant?

b) How would a nation's standard of living be affected if each nation decided to be completely self-reliant?

3. a) Name some goods or services that are traded internationally.

b) Name some goods or services that are not traded internationally.

c) What are some differences between goods and services that are traded and goods and services that are not traded?

4. According to Section 1.2 of the Salvatore text, what is a major globalization challenge?

Part One: International Trade Theory

Chapter 2
Comparative Advantage

Chapter Outline

Chapter Summary and Review

The focus of this chapter is primarily on **comparative advantage**. It is crucial to learn the ideas behind comparative advantage now because it is the reason why nations trade with each other and, consequently, is the foundation for much of what follows in subsequent chapters.

Mercantilism

For historical perspective, it is useful to begin by reviewing the views of **mercantilists'** on international trade. Mercantilism is the set of economic policies established by the writings of influential bankers, merchants, government officials and philosophers in the seventeenth and eighteenth centuries. Although there is not a set of definitive mercantilist policies, there are common elements that characterize mercantilism. With respect to international trade, mercantilists believed that a nation increased its wealth by running a trade surplus – an excess of exports of goods and service over imports of goods and services. A trade surplus means that a nation would, net, earn foreign currency, which, for currencies backed by gold, would be settled in payments in gold to the trade surplus nation. The accumulation of gold was seen as an increase in wealth.

In order for a nation to accumulate gold, that nation's trading partners must lose gold (new supplies of gold from mining are small relative to the total stock of gold in existence). Thus, mercantilists viewed wealth as a fixed "pie", in that a bigger slice for one nation would mean a smaller slice for other nations. International trade was viewed as a **zero-sum game** whereby the sum of all gains and losses always equal zero. Mercantilists' policies generally favored some government control over trade to promote an export surplus in order to accumulate gold. This view is still echoed today. News reports of trade deficits are routinely broadcast as prima facie "bad", and almost every nation uses policies (tariffs, quotas, etc.) that promote exports and inhibit imports.

Absolute Advantage

It was largely in response to the mercantilists' views on international trade that Adam Smith developed his theory of **absolute advantage**. Smith viewed exports as good and viewed imports as good, despite what the relative level of exports and imports. If trade takes place willingly, then the exporting citizen must gain or the exchange would not have taken place. Similarly, the importing citizen of the other nation must have gained or the exchange would not have been taken place. Smith viewed trade as a **positive-sum game** for which the sum of the **gains from trade** netted to a positive amount. Further, not only were the net gains positive, but they were positive for each trading participant. (This says nothing about the distribution of gains, only that both gain.) Consequently, Smith promoted trade without government control to insure that international trade would take place willingly.

Smith's theory of the gains from trade based on absolute advantage can be best explained through simple examples. Assume that two nations are each capable of producing two products (bread and ale) with their labor force. The productivity of each nation's labor force in producing the two products is given in Table 2.1

Table 2.1: Units of Output per Laborer

	Nation 1	Nation 2
Bread	4	1
Ale	1	8

From Table 2.1 Nation 1 has an absolute advantage in Bread because it can produce more Bread per laborer than can Nation 2. Nation 2 has an absolute advantage in Ale, because it can produce more Ale per laborer than can Nation 1.

According to the theory of absolute advantage, it is better for Nation 1 to produce Bread and for Nation 2 to produce Ale, rather than for each nation to be self-sufficient. If Nation 1 produces Bead and Nation 2 produces Ale, then there will be more total Bread and Ale available for the world to feed itself.

This can be shown more precisely by first assuming, before any trade (self-sufficiency), that each nation produces some Bread and Ale to feed itself. Assume the same for Nation 2. We now ask what happens to the amount of Bread and Ale available as a result of each nation producing according to absolute advantage and then trading with each other.

Suppose Nation 1 and Nation 2 each shift one laborer towards the good in which it has the absolute advantage. The changes in output due this reallocation of one laborer are shown in Table 2.2.

Table 2.2: Changes in Output due to Reallocation of One Laborer

	Nation 1	Nation 2	World
Bread	+4	-1	+3
Ale	-1	+8	+7

As a result of the reallocation, there are three more units of Bread and seven more units of Ale available to the world. Thus, a reallocation of labor has increased world output, with no change in the total amount of labor used.

Now, although each nation has more of one good, each nation also has less of the other good, so neither nation is necessarily better off. Both nations, however, can be better off if they trade with each other. Assume that Nation 1 exchanges 2 units of its extra Bread for 2 units of Nation 2's extra Ale. The rate at which goods trade internationally is generally known as the **terms of trade**, for which there are a number of measures that will not be discussed here. After exchanging, the net result for both nations is as shown in Table 2.3

**Table 2.3: Change in Output After
Exchange of 2 units of Ale for 2 units of Bread and
After Reallocation of One Laborer**

	Nation 1	Nation 2
Bread	+2 (+4-2)	+1 (-1+2)
Ale	+1 (-1+2)	+6 (+8-2)

In this example an exchange of 2 units of Bread for 2 units of Ale was assumed. There are other rates at which the exchange of goods can take place that make both nations better off. Varying the rate at which goods exchange will produce different gains from trade. Note that the net gains from reallocation and exchange are equal to the world gains in production in Table 2.2. The terms of trade of 2-for-2 produced a sharing of these gains. Different terms of trade will produce a different sharing of gains.

Comparative Advantage

The units of output per laborer for Bread and Ale for each nation in Table 2.1 were constructed such that each nation has an absolute advantage in one of the two goods. This begs the question of what happens when one nation has an absolute advantage in both goods, as is shown in Table 2.4.

Table 2.4: Units Output per Laborer

	Argentina	Haiti
Milk	6	1
Honey	2	1

Argentina has the absolute advantage in both goods, but David Ricardo showed that it is **comparative advantage** that determines trade patterns between nations. Although Argentina can produce more Milk and more Honey per laborer than Haiti, Argentina's absolute advantage in the two goods is not the same. Argentina can produce 6 times as much Milk, but only 2 times as much Honey. Similarly, Haiti has an absolute disadvantage in both goods, but the disadvantage is smaller in Honey.

If Argentina produced 2 units of honey, there would be a loss of 6 units of Milk. If, however, Haiti produced 2 units of Honey, there would be a loss of only 2 units of Milk. Because Argentina is so good (relative to Haiti) at Milk production, if Argentina produced Honey there would be a much greater loss of Milk than if Haiti produced Honey. Consequently, Argentina has a comparative advantage in the production of Milk and Haiti has a comparative advantage in the production of Honey.

Argentina's comparative advantage can be identified in this case by simply identifying where Argentina's absolute advantage is the greatest: 6-to-1 in Milk, but only 2-to-1 in Honey. Alternatively, Haiti's weakness is less in Honey, so Haiti has a comparative advantage in Honey.

To demonstrate that the world can be better off if each nation **specializes** in the good in which it has a comparative advantage, reallocate labor in each country to see the effect on world production. Assume that Argentina reallocates 1 laborer from Honey production to Milk production and Haiti reallocates three laborers from Milk production to Honey production. The effect on output is given in Table 2.4.

Table 2.5: Output Changes Due to Labor Reallocation
Haiti: Reallocation of 3 Laborers to Honey Production
Argentina: Reallocation of 1 Laborer to Milk Production

	Argentina	Haiti	World
Change in Milk Available	+6	-3	+3
Change in Honey Available	-2	+3	+1

As in the case of specializing according to absolute advantage, each nation has less of one good, but more of another, so they are not unambiguously better off. However, because there is more of both goods in the world, this extra production can be shared in a way to make both nations better off. That is to say, there is a rate at which the goods can be traded internationally to make both nations clearly better off. One such rate is 4 units of Milk for 2 units of Honey. The effect of exchanging 4 units of Milk for 2 units of Honey is shown in Table 2.6.

Table 2.6: Change in Output After Exchange of 4 units of Milk for 2 units of Honey

	Argentina	Haiti
Milk	+2(6-4)	+1(-3+4)
Honey	0(-2+2)	+1(3-2)

After the exchange, as shown in Table 2.6, Argentina has more Milk than before and just as much Honey, so Argentina is clearly better off. Haiti has 1 more unit of both goods, so Haiti is clearly better off. Consequently:

Two nations can engage in mutually beneficial trade if they specialize according to comparative advantage, even if one nation has an absolute advantage in both goods.

Comparative Advantage, Wages, and Prices

The above analysis of comparative of advantage was conducted in terms of output per laborer. It is instructive to introduce wages and prices to see how the above arguments are affected. Given the wage rate, there will be some price for each good, based on labor productivity. Using the output per laborer figures from Table 2.4, if, for example, the wage rate in Haiti is 2, then the price of Milk in Haiti will be 2. (The Haitian currency is the Gourde) If the wage rate in Haiti is 2, and one laborer can produce 1 unit of Milk, then Milk will have a price of 2. Similarly, the price of Honey in Haiti is 2. (It is assumed that markets are competitive, in which case the price equals the amount paid to the factors of production. In these simple cases, labor is the only input so if a laborer earns 2 and produces one unit of a good, the price of the good will is 2.) Similarly, given some wage rate in Argentina, there will be some prices of goods (expressed in pesos, the Argentinean currency). Whatever the wages and prices in Haiti and Argentina, suppose that price of Milk and Honey are both lower in Argentina when converted by the exchange rate into pesos or into Gourdes.

Thus, we assume some wage that produces cheaper prices in Argentina than Haiti, no matter what currency we use. This would seem to violate the law of comparative advantage because Argentina can produce both goods more cheaply.

Although this is possible, it is a disequilibrium state that will soon change. With trade Haiti will switch its demand to Argentinean goods, which along with Argentinean demand, will cause wages and prices in Argentina to increase and Haitian wages and prices to fall. Wages and prices will increase in Argentina relative to Haiti until Haiti becomes competitive (if not, then demand will still be directed towards Argentina, causing wages and prices to continue to change.) As prices and wages in Argentina increase and those in Haiti fall, Haiti will first become competitive in Honey because Haitian productivity in Honey is closer to Argentinean productivity, so the difference in prices will be smaller for this good. (This section that includes wages and prices should be reread after working through problems provided after this Discussion and Summary section.)

The consequence is that a nation with low wages and prices will not perpetually out-compete a nation with high wages prices. The low wage and price nation will experience high demand, causing wages and prices to increase, while the high price nation will experience low demand, causing wages and prices to fall. In equilibrium, nations like Mexico will not out-compete nations like Japan, German and the US. If Mexico, due to low wages out-competes the US in all goods, then the demand for Mexican goods would drive up Mexican prices and wages, reducing Mexican competitiveness. In equilibrium, Mexico and the US will produce goods in which they have a comparative advantage.

Opportunity Cost

The basic comparative advantage theory of trade can be expressed in terms of **opportunity cost**. *The opportunity cost of producing a good is the amount foregone in order to produce one unit.* Return to Table 2.4, which is reproduced below.

Table 2.4: Units Output per Laborer - Reproduced

	Argentina	Haiti
Milk	6	1
Honey	2	1

If Argentina produces 2 units of Honey, they must give up 6 units of Milk, or halving these numbers, 1 unit of Honey requires the sacrifice of 3 units of Milk. This can be written as

$$\text{Opportunity Cost of Honey in Argentina} = \frac{\Delta\text{Milk}}{\Delta\text{Honey}} = \frac{6}{2} = 3.$$

The opportunity cost of 1 more unit of Honey is 3 (less units of milk).

For Haiti, the opportunity cost of Honey is 1, which is less than Argentina's opportunity cost of 2. The production of Honey will cost the world less Milk if Haiti produces Honey, thus Haiti has a comparative advantage in Honey, just as we identified earlier by looking at the degree of absolute advantage that Argentina has in Milk and Honey relative to Haiti.

For Milk, Argentina's opportunity cost is 1/3, while the opportunity cost of Milk in Haiti is 1. The production of Milk will cost the world less Honey if Argentina produces Milk, thus Argentina has a comparative advantage in Milk, also as previously identified.

Note that the opportunity cost of Milk is just the inverse of the opportunity cost of Honey. Thus, if one nation has a comparative advantage in one good, the other nation must have a comparative advantage in the other good. Symbolically, letting M=units of Milk and H=units of Honey:

$$\text{If } (\Delta M/\Delta H)_{Haiti} < (\Delta M/\Delta H)_{Argentina} \text{ then } (\Delta H/\Delta M)_{Haiti} > (\Delta H/\Delta M)_{Argentina}.$$

Inverting an inequality reverses the inequality. If Haiti has a comparative advantage in Honey (lower opportunity cost), then Argentina must have a comparative advantage in Milk.

The only case in which a country does not have a comparative advantage would be when opportunity costs are identical in the two countries. Here, neither nation has a comparative advantage over the other.

Key Terms used in Chapter Summary and Review
(The list below is not necessarily the same as the list provided by the Salvatore text.)

Absolute Advantage
Comparative Advantage
Gains From Trade
Mercantilists
Positive-Sum Game

Specialize (Specialization)
Terms of Trade
Opportunity Cost
Zero-Sum Game

Multiple Choice Questions

1. Mercantilists' recommended trade policies intended to produce which of the following?
a) Specialization according to absolute advantage.
b) Specialization according to comparative advantage.
c) An export deficit.
d) A gold inflow.

2. If Nation 1 has an absolute advantage in two goods relative to Nation 2, and the absolute advantage is not the same for both goods, then
a) Nation 1 will have a comparative advantage in both goods.
b) Nation 2 will have an absolute advantage in one good.
c) Nation 1 will have a comparative advantage in only one good.
d) Mutually beneficial trade cannot occur.

3. If Nation 1 has an absolute advantage in one good and Nation 2 has an absolute advantage in a different good, then
a) Comparative advantage will be the same as the absolute advantage.
b) Neither nation will have a comparative advantage.
c) Comparative advantage cannot be determined.
d) Gains from trade cannot occur.

4. If the opportunity cost of producing Computers is equal to 4 in Nation 1 and is equal to 2 in Nation 2, then it is necessarily true that
a) Nation 1 has an absolute advantage in Computers.
b) Nation 2 has an absolute advantage in Computers.
c) Nation 1 has a comparative advantage in Computers
d) Nation 2 has a comparative advantage in Computers.

5. If Nation 1 can produce twice as many Autos per laborer as Nation 2, and Nation 2 can produce one-half as many DVD players per laborer as Nation 1, then
a) The opportunity cost of producing DVD players is lower in Nation 2.
b) The opportunity cost of producing autos is higher in Nation 1.
c) Nation 2 must have an absolute advantage in DVD players.
d) Neither nation has a comparative advantage in DVD players.

6. In Nation 1 the opportunity cost of producing 1 unit of Soup is 4 units of Nuts. In Nation 2 the opportunity cost of producing 1 unit of Soup is 1 Nut. Nation 1 will be able to gain from trade with Nation 2 if the terms of trade are
a) 6 Nuts for 1 Soup.
b) 5 Nuts for 1 Soup.
c) 4 Nuts for 1 Soup.
d) 3 Nuts for 1 Soup.

7. The wage rate in Nation H is $4 per laborer and output per laborer in Nation H is 8 units of Cheese. The wage rate in Nation L is $1 per laborer and output per laborer in Nation L is 1 unit of Cheese. Which of the following must be true at these wage rates and productivity levels?
a) Nation L will out-compete nation H in the production of Cheese.
b) The price of Cheese in Nation H will be $0.50 and the price of Cheese in Nation L will be $1.
c) The price of Cheese in Nation H will be $2 and the price of Cheese in Nation L will be 1.
d) As a result of its lower wage rate, Nation L must have an absolute advantage in the production of Cheese.

8. If Egypt has wage rates so low that the prices of the goods it trades with Germany are lower than Germany's prices, then
a) Germans will buy all of these goods from Egypt for the foreseeable future.
b) Egyptians will buy all of these goods from Germany for the foreseeable future.
c) Germany's prices will eventually fall relative to Egypt's and trade will occur.
d) Germany's prices will eventually increase relative to Egypt's and trade will occur.

9. The mercantilists' view on trade is implies which of the following?
a) Gains from trade in one nation mean a net loss to that nation's trading partners.
b) All nations could simultaneously experience a gold inflow.
c) Nations always gain from trade.
d) Trade is a positive-sum game.

10. If two nations have the same opportunity costs for two goods, then it must be the case that
a) Neither has an absolute advantage in either good.
b) One nation will have a comparative advantage in one of the goods.
c) Trade can occur at the right terms of trade.
d) Neither nation has a comparative advantage in either good.

Problems and Discussion Questions

1. The output per laborer in the production of candles and incense for Thailand and Cambodia are given in the table below.

Output per Laborer

	Thailand	Cambodia
Candles	1	4
Incense	3	4

a) Which nation has the absolute advantage in each good?

b) Which nation has the comparative advantage in each good?

c) Assume that Thailand transfers 2 laborers to the product of its comparative advantage, and Cambodia transfers 1 laborer to the product of its comparative advantage. Complete the table below.

Changes in Production from Reallocating Two Units of Labor

	Thailand	Cambodia	World
Change in Candles	−2	(1×4)=4	2
Change in Incense	(2×3)=6	−4	2

d) Will Thailand trade if 3 units of Incense can be traded for 1 or less units of Candles?

e) Will Cambodia trade if 4 units of Candles can be traded for 4 or less units of Incense?

f) Will Cambodia and Thailand trade if 6 units of Incense can be traded for 4 units of Candles?

g) Based on your answers to parts (d), (e) and (f), summarize what the terms of trade must be in order for two nations to gain from trade.

2. The table below gives the number of labor-hours required by two nations to produce one unit of each good indicated.

Labor-hours Required Per Unit of Output

	Upland	Overland
Good A	1	4
Good E	4	1

a) Which nation has the absolute advantage in each good?

b) Which nation has the comparative advantage in each good?

3. The output per laborer per day in the production of steel and tin for Russia and China are given in the table below.

Output per Labor-Day

	Russia	China
Steel	10	3
Tin	5	6

a) What is the opportunity cost of producing Tin in Russia?

b) What is the opportunity cost of producing Tin in China?

c) Assume that Russia has 500 labor days available for producing Steel and/or Tin, and that China has 900 labor days available. Putting Steel on the vertical axis, draw the straight-line production possibility frontiers for both Russia and China.

d) What is the slope of Russia's production possibility frontier, and what is the slope of China's production possibility frontier?

e) How is the slope of a production possibility frontier related to the opportunity cost of the good on the horizontal axis? (See your answers to parts (a) and (b) of this question.)

f) What does a straight-line production possibility frontier imply?

g) Which country will specialize in and export Tin?

h) What is a possible terms of trade at which both nations will be willing to trade?

i) Plot a terms of trade line at which both nations will be willing to trade on your production possibility frontiers of part (c), starting the terms of trade line from a point of complete specialization for each nation.

j) How does your diagram from part (i) demonstrate how nations gain from trade?

4. Use the table of output per labor-day from Question 3.
a) Fill in the table below, assuming that the wage rate in Russia, expressed in dollars, is $10 per day, and that the wage rate in China, expressed in dollars, is $6 per day.

Price of Steel and China

	Russia	China
Price of Steel	___	___
Price of Tin	___	___

b) Based on your table values from part (a), does the nation with the lower wage always have the lower price?

c) Other than wages, what determines prices?

d) Assume now that the wage rate in Russia is $10 per day, as before, but the wage rate in China is $1. Could these be equilibrium wage rates?

5. Two nations have straight-line production possibility frontiers, but with different slopes. Explain or demonstrate why complete specialization maximizes the gains from trade.

6. The models of trade developed in this chapter used differing output per unit of labor to explain trade. What might explain why output per unit of labor varies across nations?

Chapter 3
The Standard Trade Model

Chapter Outline

Chapter Summary and Review

Increasing Costs

The Ricardian model of comparative advantage developed in Chapter 2 assumes that the number of units of output produced per laborer for each good is unchanged as total production of the good changes. If 1 laborer can produce 4 units of bread, then 2 laborers can produce 8 units of bread, 3 laborers can produce 12 units of bread, etc. Although the productivity of labor is assumed to be constant for each good, the Ricardian model assumes that the productivity of labor differs between goods and nations. These differences in productivity are the source of comparative advantage.

Using the hypothetical example in Chapter 2 of this Study Guide (Table 2.), if Argentina can produce 6 times as much Milk as Haiti but only 2 times as much Honey, then Argentina will have the comparative advantage in Milk and Haiti will have the comparative advantage in Honey. This raises the question of why the productivity of labor might differ between nations. A relatively simple answer is that there must be other factors that make labor more or less productive, such as capital, natural resources, access to education and training, etc.

If the productivity of labor is constant for each good then Chapter 2 of the Salvatore text shows that the production possibility frontier (ppf) will be linear with a slope equal to the opportunity cost of the good on the horizontal axis. The inverse of the slope is the opportunity cost of the good on the vertical axis. If other factors of production, such as capital and natural resources, are added to the analysis, then a reallocation of factors from one product to another will generally not produce constant costs. One possibility is **increasing costs**. As the production of one good decreases factors are released that can be used in the production of the other good. This produces some tradeoff. If the tradeoff is pursued further, the factors that are transferred will not be as productive if it is assumed that the more transferable factors were reallocated first. If, for example, bread production is decreased it will release some factors that can be used to produce honey. Bread production will, presumably, be decreased where it is produced by factors most conducive to honey production. If bread production is decreased again, then the factors released will be somewhat less productive than for the first reduction in bread production. This implies that as bread production is continually decreased the additional units honey possible will be smaller and smaller.

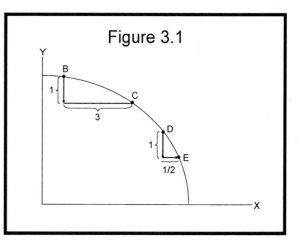

Figure 3.1

A ppf with increasing costs is shown in Figure 3.1. If production moves from point B to point C, then the opportunity cost of one unit of good X is

$$(\Delta Y/\Delta X)=1/3.$$

One less unit of Y releases enough resources to produce three more units of X.

Now consider the opportunity cost of X at point D, a higher level of production of X than at point B. If production moves from point D to point E, then the opportunity cost of one unit of good X is

$$(\Delta Y/\Delta X)=1/0.5 = 2$$

On less unit of Y now releases enough resources to produce only ½ unit of X. As more X is produced, the opportunity cost of producing one unit of good X increases.

In Fig. 3.1 the opportunity cost of good X is the change in Y divided by the change in X. This is just the slope of the ppf. (If Y were on the horizontal axis, the slope would be the opportunity cost of good Y.) This slope, ignoring negative signs, is called the **marginal rate of transformation** of good Y into X and can be written as $MRT_{Y/X}$. In Fig. 3.1, increasing costs is equivalent to saying that $MRT_{Y/X}$ increases as the production of good X increases. In order to produce a unit of X at higher levels of production of X, more Y must be given up than at lower levels of production of X.

Community Indifference Curves

The ppf describes possible levels of production. The level of production chosen by the community depends upon the community's preferences, which are characterized diagrammatically by **community indifference curves**, sometimes called "**preference maps**." Indifference curves show combinations of goods to which the community is indifferent. Given indifferent combinations, superior and inferior combinations can be easily determined.

There are some basic properties of indifference curves, some of which are reviewed here. First, because the well-being of the community is unchanged along (on) indifference curves, indifference curves must be downward sloping in X,Y space. If X and Y are goods, in that more is better, then if some of one good is taken away from the community, then some amount of another good must be added in order to maintain the same level of well being. This negative slope is the rate at which one good can be substituted for another to produce equally valued combinations of X and Y. The slope, $\Delta Y / \Delta X$ (if X is on the horizontal axis) in absolute value, is known as the **marginal rate of substitution**, and can be written as $MRS_{Y/X}$. If $MRS_{Y/X}=4$, then four units of Y are necessary to just compensate for one unit of X, or equivalently, one more unit of X will just compensate for the loss of four units of Y.

Second, as more of a good is consumed, it is reasonable to assume that each additional unit of the good adds to well-being, but by a smaller amount than previous units. (The third ice-cold soft drink on a hot and humid day is probably not as satisfying as the first or second drink.) This is described as the phenomenon of "diminishing marginal utility." This means that at higher levels of consumption of X, smaller increases in Y will be necessary to compensate for a loss of one unit of X. This means the $MRS_{Y/X}$ decreases (in absolute value) as X is increased. Because the MRS is the slope the slope gets flatter as X is increased.

These two properties are exhibited in Figure 3.2. Referring to the indifference curve labeled I_1, the line is downward sloping and the slope gets smaller (in absolute) value as consumption of X increases from point F to point G.

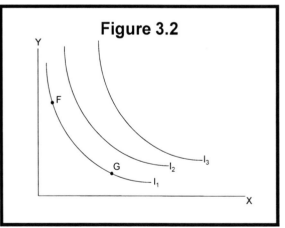

Figure 3.2

A third property is that for every X,Y combination there is some level of preference as indicated by the indifference curve passing through that combinations. Thus, every point in X,Y space falls on some indifference curve.

A fourth property is that if more is better, then indifference curves to the northeast indicate superior combinations. For example, I_2 is superior to indifference curve I_1 because there are points on I_2 that have both more Y and more X. If every point on I_2 is equivalent, then all points on I_2 are superior to all points on I_1. Each indifference curve represents some level of satisfaction, synonyms for which are "welfare", "well being", and "utility". I_1 represents some measure of welfare and I_2 represents a higher level of welfare.

Finally, each point in X,Y space produces one unique level of well being, so two indifference curves cannot pass through one point, or indifference curves cannot intersect.

Equilibrium in Isolation

Given what's possible as described by the ppf and the preferences described by the community indifference curves, the optimal level of production and consumption in the absence of trade (isolation, or autarchy) can be determined. For any point on the ppf there is an indifference curve passing through that point, as is shown for point J in Figure 3.3. This is not an optimum point, however, because moving along the ppf to point K –more Y and less X- improves the community's welfare from I_1 to I_2. The objective is to produce at the point where it is not possible to change production and move to a superior indifference curve. Alternatively the objective is to find the point on the ppf that achieve the highest indifference curve. This occurs at the tangency between the ppf and an indifference as at point A. At point A, the slopes of the ppf and indifference curve are equal, so $MRT_{Y/X}=MRS_{Y/X}$. In the absence of trade, an economy will choose to produce at point A (autarchy).

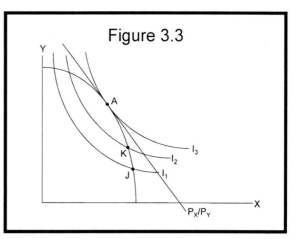

Figure 3.3

Note that at the optimum autarchy point, the amounts produced and the amounts consumed are identical. In autarchy a nation's consumption is limited to its own production. In the absence of trade a nation is self dependent.

The slope of the ppf at point A represents the opportunity cost of good X. It is the amount of X that can be had by giving up some amount of Y. For example, if the slope is $\Delta Y/\Delta X=3/1$, then one X can be had by giving up three Y's. This implies that the price of X is three times that of Y, or $P_X/P_Y=3/1$. Goods will exchange in inverse ratio to the relative price. The slope of the tangency at point A represents the price of X relative to Y in autarchy, and is labeled as such in Fig. 3.3.

Trade in the Increasing Cost Model

Trade will occur if two nations have different relative prices in autarchy. Suppose that autarchy occurs in two nations where the relative prices differ, say,

$$\left(\frac{P_X}{P_Y}\right)_1 < \left(\frac{P_X}{P_Y}\right)_2$$

The subscripts "1" and "2" indicate, respectively, nations 1 and 2. The above inequality says that the price of good X, relative to the price of good Y, is lower in Nation 1 than Nation 2, so Nation 1 has the comparative advantage in good X. If both sides of the inequality is inverted (which causes the inequality to reverse), it says that the price of good Y, relative to the price of good X is lower in Nation 2, so Nation 2 has a comparative advantage in good Y.

The effect of trade is shown in Figure 3.4 for Nation 1 with a comparative advantage in good X. As Nation 1 specializes in good X, the relative price of X will increase (its opportunity cost increases along the ppf). As Nation 2 (not shown) specializes in the production of good Y, it will produce less X so the relative price of good X will fall in Nation 2. At some point the increasing relative price of good X in Nation 1 will meet the falling relative price of good X in Nation 2. This is assumed to be the equilibrium price ratio shown in Fig. 3.4 as $(P_X/P_Y)_e$.

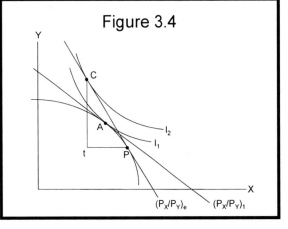

Figure 3.4

At the terms of trade shown in Fig. 3.4, Nation 1 will produce at point P and trade off along the equilibrium price ratio line until the highest indifference curve can be reached, which occurs at point C where the indifference curve is tangent to the equilibrium price ratio line. Point C is Nation 1's optimum consumption point when trade is possible at the indicated equilibrium price ratio. Nation 1 moves from point P by exporting X and importing Y. The quantity exported of X is equal to the distance tP and the quantity imported of Y is equal to the distance tC. The triangle PtC is known as the **trading triangle**.

As a result of trade a nation is able to consume outside its own ppf. The equilibrium price ratio line in Fig. 3.4 represents the amounts that Nation 1 can consume through trading and it lies outside the nation's ppf. Because that line represents possible levels of consumption it is sometimes called the **consumption possibility frontier**. The **gains from trade** are measured by the increase in well-being made possible through trade. At autarchy, the best Nation 1 could achieve is I_1. After trade Nation 1 can achieve I_2, so the gains from trade are I_2-I_1. Trade allows a nation to consume a combination of goods superior (on a higher indifference curve) than that which is available without trade.

Equilibrium Price Ratio and the Terms of Trade

The equilibrium price ratio with trade in Fig. 3.4, $(P_X/P_Y)_e$, was assumed. The determination of the equilibrium price ratio with trade can be shown with standard supply and demand curves.

At autarchy, each nation is self-sufficient so there is no world supply or demand for good X. With trade, Nation 1, the low-price producer of good X, will be the exporter of good X at the higher relative prices that Nation 2 will be willing to pay, as long as the new relative price is below Nation 2's high relative price of X. (This suggests that trade will generally occur at prices between those of the trading countries.)

As the relative price of X increases for Nation 1, Nation 1 will produce more X and consume less, creating domestic excess supply available for export. As the price increases further there will be even greater excess supply as production further increases and consumption decreases more, creating an even greater quantity supplied of X for export. The supply curve for exports of X to the world market by Nation 1 is shown in Figure 3.5 as S_{X1}.

Because Nation 2 can buy good X from Nation 1 at a price lower than Nation 2 can produce it at, there will be a demand for good X from Nation 2. This demand for X by Nation 2 is the amount of X that Nation 2 wants to import from Nation 1. How much Nation 2 wants to import depends on the price. As the relative price of X at

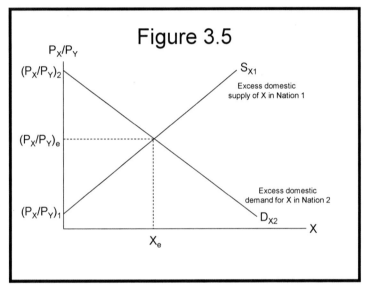

which Nation 2 can buy X falls, Nation 2 will produce less X and consume more X, which creates an increased quantity demanded of imports of X from Nation 1. The demand curve for imports by Nation 2 is shown in Fig. 3.5 as D_{X2}.

Note that at Nation 2's autarchy price ratio of $(P_X/P_Y)_2$ there is no excess demand for good X from Nation 2. At autarchy, domestic producers fulfill domestic demand, so there is no excess demand for X on the world market. Similarly, there is no domestic excess supply in Nation 1 at Nation 1's autarchy price of $(P_X/P_Y)_1$. At the equilibrium price of $(P_X/P_Y)_e$, the amount of X that Nation 1 wants to export equals X_e, which is also the amount of X that Nation 2 wants to import. Also recognize that X_e equals the distance tP in Fig. 3.4.

In a two-nation world, the **terms of trade** are simply the ratio of the price of exports to the price of imports. In the example above, $(P_X/P_Y)_e$ is the terms of trade for Nation 1 because X is Nation 1's export good and Y is Nation 1's import good. For

Nation 2, the terms of trade would just be the inverse of Nation 1's terms of trade for one nation's imports are the other's exports.

In a multi-nation world, the terms of trade are expressed as the ratio of a price index of exports to a price index of imports. A price index is simply a way to measure the average price of goods.

In most conditions, an increase in the terms of trade is favorable for it means an increase in the price of exports relative to the price of import. An increase in the terms of trade means that more goods can be imported for a given unit of exports. If, for example the terms of trade are 1/1, then a unit of exports yields enough revenues to buy one unit of imports. If the terms of trade increase to 2/1, then a unit of exports yields enough revenues to buy two units of imports. A doubling in the terms of trade means a doubling in the purchasing power of exports.

Key Terms used in Chapter Summary and Review
(The list below is not necessarily the same as the list provided by the Salvatore text.)

Community indifference curves (Preference maps)   Marginal rate of substitution
Consumption possibility frontier   Marginal rate of transformation
Gains from trade   Trading triangle
Increasing costs   Terms of trade

Multiple Choice Questions

1. In Figure 3.1, the opportunity cost of producing good X
a) Increases as the production of X increases.
b) Increases as the production of Y increases.
c) Decreases as the production of Y increases.
d) Remains constant as the production of good Y increases.

2. In Figure 3.1, the opportunity cost of producing good Y
a) Increases as the production of X increases.
b) Increases as the production of Y increases.
c) Decreases as the production of Y increases.
d) Remains constant as the production of good Y increases.

3. If a nation can produce three more units of X by producing one less unit of Y, then
a) $(P_X/P_Y)=1/3$
b) $\Delta Y/\Delta X = 3/1$
c) The opportunity cost of one unit of Y is one-third unit of X.
d) The opportunity cost of one unit of X is three units of Y.

4. Which of the following best characterizes the effect of trade?
a) The ppf of at least one nation must shift in.
b) One nation can gain only if another loses.
c) All nations can consume outside its ppf.
d) Nations move to a preferred position on the ppf.

5. In an increasing-cost model
a) The gains from trade are fully offset by higher costs.
b) Lower levels of production have higher opportunity cost.
c) Complete specialization is more likely than in a constant-cost model.
d) The opportunity cost of either good will increase if its production increases.

6. Given a nation's ppf, an increase in the nation's terms of trade will
a) Increase the degree of specialization.
b) Reduce the nation's gains from trade.
c) Make other nations better off.
d) Make the nation worse off.

7. Which of the following is **not** a characteristic of a community's set of indifference curves for goods?
a) They may intersect.
b) They are downward sloping.
c) The MRS changes as consumption changes.
d) They indicate opportunity cost.

8. If an exporting nation's domestic demand for the good it exports increases then based on supply and demand curves like those shown in Figure 3.4
a) Import demand increases.
b) Import demand decreases.
c) Export supply increases.
d) Export supply decreases.

9. Suppose China exports CD players and the US imports CD players. If US income increases and CD players are a normal good then based on supply and demand curves like those shown in Figure 3.4
a) The terms of trade will improve for the US.
b) The terms of trade will improve for China.
c) China will reduce its specialization in CD players.
d) The quantity of CD players traded between China and the US will decrease.

10. If a nation's opportunity cost of producing one unit of X is 1 unit of Y, and the world equilibrium price ratio is $(P_X/P_Y)=2$, then the nation will
a) Specialize in good X.
b) Specialize in good Y.
c) Export good Y.
d) Import good X.

Problems and Discussion Questions

1. a) With Y on the vertical axis and X on the horizontal axis, draw a country that is producing in autarky where its community indifference curve is steeper than its production possibility frontier.

b) What is the $MRS_{Y/x}$ relative to the opportunity cost of X?
   $MRS_{y/x} > MRT$
c) Should the country produce more of good X or less of good X?

d) At equilibrium, what is the relationship between the number of units the community will give up for X and the opportunity cost of X? Equal

2. a) Suppose in autarchy that Midland and Zeeland have the following price ratios for Chicken (C) and Noodles (N).

$$Midland: P_C/P_N=4/1$$
$$Zeeland: P_C/P_N=1/2.$$

b) What is the range of relative prices for which Zeeland willingly specializes in and exports Chicken?

c) What is the range of relative prices for which Midland willingly specializes in and exports Noodles?

d) What is the range or prices for which both a) and b) is true?

e) Assume a relative price within the range given in d) and graphically show for each if the following for Midland.
   i)   Autarchy equilibrium. Label it A.
   ii)   The production point after trade. Label it P.
   iii)   The consumption point after trade. Label it C.
   iv)   Exports. Show the distance.
   v)   Imports. Show the distance.
   vi)   Gains from trade.

3. Is complete specialization more or less likely if production possibility frontiers exhibit increasing costs rather than constant costs?

4. a) A nation exports baseballs and imports baseball bats. Show this graphically using ppfs, community indifference curves, and relative price lines. Measure the number of baseballs on the vertical axis and the number of bats on the horizontal axis.

b) Using your graph from a), demonstrate how the welfare of this nation is affected by a decrease in the price of baseballs relative to baseball bats.

5. a) Could two nations beneficially trade crackers and cheese if they have identical preference maps for crackers and cheese?

b) Could two nations beneficially trade crackers and cheese if they have identical production possibility frontiers for crackers and cheese?

c) Could two nations beneficially trade crackers and cheese if they have both identical preference maps and ppfs for crackers and cheese?

Chapter 4
The Heckscher-Ohlin and Other Trade Theories

Chapter Outline

Chapter Summary and Review

Mutually beneficial trade can occur between nations when there is a difference in pre-trade relative prices. Whereas Chapter 3 established that mutually beneficial trade could take place when relative prices differ across nations, this chapter offers explanations as to why pre-trade relative prices differ across nations.

Heckscher-Ohlin Theory

The Heckscher-Ohlin (H-O) theory is based on the relative supplies of the factors of production in each nation, assuming that the relative demand for products is identical in each nation. The H-O theory is also known as the **factor endowments theory,** or **factor proportions theory.**

For simplicity, assume only two factors of production, capital (K) and labor (L); two products, Y and X; and two nations, Nation 1 and Nation 2. In the H-O model, goods X and Y are classified according to their factor intensity, meaning goods are classified as either capital intensive or labor intensive. If good Y is capital intensive it means that good Y uses more capital *relative* to labor than good X, i.e.,

$$(K/L)_Y > (K/L)_X.$$

This relative definition means that good X could use more capital than good Y, but if the ratio of capital to labor is higher in good Y, then good Y is capital intensive. Note that if good Y is capital intensive, then good X must necessarily be labor intensive. (Inverting the above inequality reverses the inequality producing $(L/K)_Y < (L/K)_X$.)

Now suppose that nations can be classified according to their factor abundance, and that that Nation 2 is capital abundant (capital rich) relative to Nation 1. In the H-O model this means that the ratio of the supply of capital to the supply of labor in Nation 2 exceeds that of Nation 1. This can be written as

$$(K/L)_2 > (K/L)_1.$$

As with factor intensity, factor abundance is a relative concept. Nation 2 may have more or less capital than Nation 1, but if it is capital abundant then Nation 2 will have greater capital relative to labor than Nation 1. If Nation 2 is capital abundant, then Nation 1 is necessarily labor abundant. (Inverting the above inequality reverses the inequality producing $(L/K)_2 < (L/K)_1$.)

If relative factor abundances differ then the cost of using labor (the real wage rate-w) relative to the cost of using capital (the real interest rate-r) will differ between the two nations. If Nation 1 is labor abundant, then $(w/r)_1 < (w/r)_2$, and $(r/w)_1 > (r/w)_2$.

Because Nation 2 is capital rich and good Y is capital intensive, Nation 2 will have a lower opportunity cost of good Y, for given levels of production than Nation 1. Nation 1 will have a lower opportunity cost of good X for a given level of production. The slopes of the production possibility frontiers in Figure 4.1 demonstrate the opportunity costs in each nation.

At the same value of X in each nation, X_a, Nation 1's production possibility frontier (ppf) is flatter than Nation 2's ppf. Comparing the slopes at points D and E,

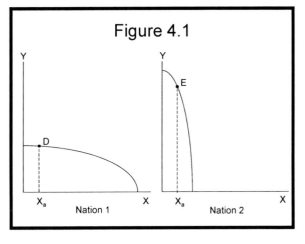

Figure 4.1

$$\text{(Opportunity Cost of X)}_1 < \text{Opportunity Cost of X)}_2$$

and

$$(P_X/P_Y)_1 < (P_X/P_Y)_2.$$

This also means

$$\text{(Opportunity Cost of Y)}_1 > \text{Opportunity Cost of Y)}_2$$

and

$$(P_Y/P_X)_1 > (P_Y/P_X)_2.$$

If the demands for products are identical in each nation, or not so different as to offset the price differences above, then price differences between the two nations in autarky will be due to different ppfs, which are due to factor supplies.

Based on the ppfs above, then, Nation 1 will have a comparative advantage in X and Nation 2 will have a comparative advantage in Y. This is an example of the **Heckscher-Ohlin Theorem** which states:

> *A nation will have a comparative advantage in*
> *the good that uses its abundant factors intensely.*

Given a nation's comparative advantage, trade can be shown graphically as in Chapter 3. The equilibrium relative commodity prices with trade will lie in between the two nation's ppfs. Each nation will export the good described by the Heckscher-Ohlin Theorem, and import the other good.

Trade and Factor Prices

Prior to trade, relative factor prices (w/r) will differ, which causes relative prices to differ and leads to trade. Continuing with the example from above,

$$(w/r)_1 < (w/r)_2.$$

As a result of trade between the two nations, the return to labor -the wage rate- and the return to capital –the interest rate- will change. Nation 1 with cheap labor and a comparative advantage in labor-intensive good X will produce more of good X in response to the demand for good X from Nation 2. As Nation 1 produces more of labor-intensive good X and less of capital-intensive good Y, the demand for labor will increase and the demand for capital will decrease. Thus trade causes $(w/r)_1$ to increase. The opposite occurs in Nation 2 as it produces more of the capital-intensive good. This causes the w/r ratio of each nation to move that of the other nation.

Further, because any difference between relative factor prices will mean a difference in relative prices, factor prices must equalize. If they did not, then relative prices would differ and trade would expand further. Trade equalizes prices at the international price ratio and so equalizes relative factor prices. The equalization of the wage-rental ratio is called **relative factor-price equalization**.

This same process occurs for absolute factor prices. If wages or the interest rate differed between nations, then absolute prices would differ and trade would differ and trade would expand until they and factor prices were equalized. This is **absolute factor-price equalization**.

Factor price equalization, relative and absolute, only applies to factors that are the same. Wages will only be equalized across factors that are the same in each country. Thus, the wages of all computer programmers will not be equalized across nations; the wages of equally expert computer programmers will be equalized across all nations. Like in a competitive domestic economy, the wages of workers with identical skill levels in jobs with identical characteristics will be equalized.

Factor-price equalization implies that the distribution of income within countries will change as a result of trade. In capital-rich nations, trade lowers the wage rate and increases the interest rate. In labor-rich nations, trade increases the wage rate and lowers the interest rate. This is an example of the **Stolper-Samuelson Theorem** which states that trade increases the real return to a nation's abundant factor and decreases the real return to the nation's scarce factor. Although there are gains to some groups and losses to others, the net effect is an increase in income because trade allows nations to consume outside their production possibility frontiers.

Both factor-price equalization and the Stolper-Samuelson Theorem apply when factors are mobile *within* each nation. In the short-run, factors are less mobile, especially capital. If, in response to trade, capital does not move out of the sector competing with imports into the export sector, then returns on capital within the nation will not be equalized. The returns to capital in the expanding export sector will increase, while returns to capital in the contracting import-competing sector will decrease. The effect on labor is indeterminate. (This is described in Appendix A4.1. of the Salvatore textbook.) In the short run, trade may not increase a nation's income. In the long run, however, all factors are mobile and trade enhances the ability of each nation to consume.

The long-run effect of trade on factor prices in the H-O model (factor-price equalization) is identical to the effect on factor prices from the movement of factors across countries. For example, labor from labor-rich nations with low wages emigrates to labor-scarce nations with high wages. Without trade, the pressure for factors to move across borders will be higher than if the factor-equalizing effect of trade is allowed to occur.

Extensions and Alternatives to the Heckscher-Ohlin Model

In 1951 economist Vassily Leontief found that for 1947, the US, which was clearly labor-rich relative to other nations, exported labor-intensive goods and imported capital-intensive goods. This is in direct contradiction to the H-O model and so is called the **Leontief Paradox**. This paradox has led to extensions of the H-O model as well as the development of alternative models.

The H-O model has been extended to include physical capital, natural resources, and various classifications of labor, which is a distinct improvement over the simple classification into physical capital and labor. When factors are more appropriately classified, the H-O model becomes an appropriate explanation of many trade patterns and the effect of trade on incomes. Although the H-O model does explain many trade patterns, there are other forms of trade that are not based on differences in factor endowments.

In the H-O model, costs increase as each good's production increases. If, however, there are increasing returns to scale then costs per unit will decrease as production increases. Increasing returns to scale can be due to the greater possible levels of specialization of resources at higher levels of production. If there are increasing returns to scale the ppf is convex from below, as demonstrated in Figure 4.2.

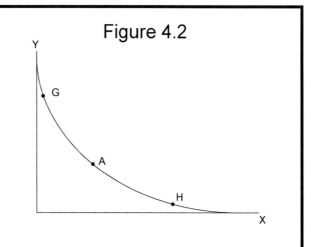

The steepness of the ppf in Fig. 4.2 represents the opportunity cost of X. At point G the ppf is quite steep, indicating a high opportunity cost of X. At a higher level of production of X, as at point H, the ppf is relatively flat, indicating a low opportunity cost of X. (The same holds true for Y. As production of Y increases, the opportunity cost (inverse steepness of the ppf in Fig. 4.2) of producing Y decreases.

With increasing returns it is not necessary for trade to begin with each country having a comparative advantage in a good, as in the H-O case. Suppose that both nations are producing at point A in Fig. 4.2. Neither will have a comparative advantage because both will have the same opportunity cost. If one nation, for whatever reason, begins to produce more of good X, then the opportunity cost of good X for that nation will fall. As the nation produces more X because the other nation will demand it at the lower cost/price, the opportunity cost will fall further. This will continue until the nation is completely specialized in producing good X. As the other nation produces less X and more Y, the cost of Y will continually drop until the other nation completely specializes in the production of Y.

Note two interesting things about how trade develops with increasing returns to scale. First, a nation acquires a comparative advantage in a product by producing more of the product rather than through some other characteristic of the nation, such as factor endowments in the H-O model. Second, because of the first point, either nation can have a comparative advantage in either product (but not both).

In the H-O model, a nation exports one product and imports a different product. This is called **inter-industry trade**. Although there is substantial inter-industry trade in the world, **intra-industry trade** is also very important. Intra-industry trade occurs where the goods a nation exports and imports are in the same industry, but are slightly differentiated. Such **product differentiation** is a characteristic of trade in cheese, wine, autos and a host of other products.

When consumers like variety in products, as with cheese, wine and autos, each nation cannot competitively provide all of the varieties if there are increasing returns to scale. Increasing returns to scale requires large-scale production, which nations cannot pursue for all varieties of a good. Through time, nations will acquire expertise in certain varieties of a product (e.g., French champagne, German luxury autos, etc.) while other nations will acquire expertise in other varieties. Nations will gain by trading these varieties with each other because increasing returns to scale will lower the price of all goods. If each nation produced all of the varieties of goods it consumed, the levels of production would be lower for each, resulting in a higher price for each. (This does not mean that all intra-industry trade must be based on increasing returns to scale. It is quite probable that some trade in differentiated products is based on differences in factor endowments.)

The **product cycle model** (an outgrowth of the technological gap model) is a dynamic H-O model. High-income nations that can afford to heavily invest in education, research, and development, will enjoy a comparative advantage in technologically new products. These scientifically advanced nations will produce these new products for their own markets and for export markets. In time the technology to produce the product will become standardized and the comparative advantage will shift to lower income nations that can provide cheap assembly-line labor. Eventually the lower income nations will enjoy a comparative advantage in the product and the richer nations will be developing new products.

Key Terms used in Chapter Summary and Review
(The list below is not necessarily the same as the list provided by the Salvatore text.)

Absolute factor-price equalization	Inter-industry trade
Factor abundance	Intra-industry trade
Factor endowments theory	Leontief Paradox
Factor intensity	Product differentiation
Factor proportions theory	Product cycle model
Heckscher-Ohlin Theory	Relative factor price equalization
Heckscher-Ohlin Theorem	Stolper-Samuelson Theorem
Increasing returns to scale	

Multiple Choice Questions

1. France is necessarily capital rich if:
a) France has more capital than the US.
b) France has less labor than the US.
c) France has more capital and labor than the US.
d) France has more capital and less labor than the US.

2. If the US is capital rich relative to Greece and construction equipment is capital intensive relative to olives, then
a) Greece has a comparative advantage in olives.
b) The US should produce its own olives.
c) Greece should produce its own construction equipment.
d) The US has a comparative advantage in olives.

3. If Nation 1 has a comparative advantage in good X and Nation 2 has a comparative advantage in good Y then
a) $(P_X/P_Y)_1 > (P_X/P_Y)_2$ in autarchy.
b) $(P_X/P_Y)_1 = (P_X/P_Y)_2$ in autarchy.
c) $(P_X/P_Y)_1 = (P_X/P_Y)_2$ after trade.
d) $(P_X/P_Y)_1 > (P_X/P_Y)_2$ after trade.

4. In the H-O model, trade for a labor-rich nation will
a) Increase the returns to labor and decrease the returns to capital.
b) Decrease the returns to both labor and capital.
c) Increase the returns to both labor and capital.
d) Decrease the returns to labor and increase the returns to capital.

5. A nation's two factors are low-wage unskilled labor and high-wage skilled labor. The nation is rich in unskilled labor. As a result of trade
a) Inequality will be reduced in the nation.
b) Inequality will be increased in the nation.
c) Inequality will be unaffected in the nation.
d) The wages of both types of labor will increase.

6. Which of the following statements is an example of the Leontief Paradox?
a) A capital-rich nation exports capital-intensive products.
b) A capital-rich nation imports capital-intensive products.
c) A capital rich nation imports labor-intensive products.
d) A labor-rich nation imports capital-intensive products.

7. According to the H-O model
a) A capital-rich nation exports labor-intensive products.
b) A capital-rich nation imports capital-intensive products.
c) A capital rich nation imports labor-intensive products.
d) A labor-rich nation exports capital-intensive products.

8. If there are increasing returns to scale then
a) There will be higher levels of specialization.
b) Increases in production will increase cost.
c) It is better for a nation to produce all varieties of a product it demands.
d) trade will be inter-industry trade.

9. According to the factor-price equalization theorem, trade will equalize
a) The returns to labor and capital within a nation.
b) The wage rate among all skill levels of labor in a nation.
c) The wage rate between identical occupations across nations.
d) The prices of the same goods no matter where they are produced.

10. In the Heckscher-Ohlin model
a) Trade is intra-industry trade.
b) Trade is in differentiated products.
c) There are increasing returns to scale.
d) There are increasing costs.

Problems and Discussion Questions

1. Textiles are labor intensive and Computers are capital intensive.
a) Based on the ppfs in Figure 4.3, which nation is relatively capital abundant?

b) Does the nation you chose in part a) necessarily have more capital?

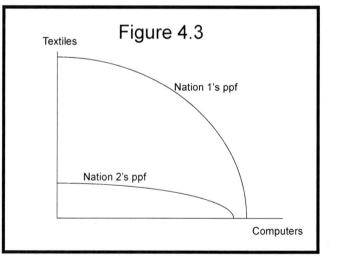

2. Use the ppf for Nation 1 in Figure 4.3 and community indifference curves to show the following.
a) A likely equilibrium in autarchy. Label it A.

b) A likely production point after trade. Label it P.

c) A likely consumption point after trade. Label it C.

d) Exports. Show the distance.

e) Imports. Show the distance.

3. In answering Question 2, what did you implicitly assume about employment before and after trade?

4. a) For which nation in Figure 4.3 is w/r higher before trade?

b) How will trade affect w/r in Nation 2?

c) Will laborers gain or lose in Nation 2?

d) Will owners of capital gain or lose in Nation 2?

5. a) Why is product differentiation by itself incapable of explaining intra-industry trade?

b) How does product differentiation combined with increasing returns to scale explain intra-industry trade?

6. Under what condition can trade occur if no nation has a comparative advantage in autarchy?

7. Suppose Japan, a capital rich nation relative to Mexico, attempts to negotiate a trade agreement promoting trade between Japan and Mexico.
a) Which group in each nation, capital or labor, is likely to resist the agreement?

b) Could the gainers possibly compensate the losers if the agreement were to pass?

8. For which of the following products would you predict the greatest level of intra-industry trade, assuming there are increasing returns to scale?
a) Common sand.

b) Wheat.

c) Children's toys.

d) Rubber bands.

Chapter 5
Trade Restrictions: Tariffs

Chapter Outline

Chapter Summary and Review

The Nature and Purpose of Tariffs

Tariffs are taxes that are imposed on nations' import goods and/or export goods, although export tariffs are not constitutional in the US. The intent of import tariffs includes protection from foreign competition and the generation of tariff revenues. In more developed economies import tariffs are primarily used to protect targeted industries from foreign competition because tariff revenues small relative to the revenues collected through taxes on income or general consumption. In developing countries tariffs are used to not only protect specific economic industries, but also as an important source of revenues. Tariffs are currently relatively low in the more developed economies, averaging well under 5%. Developing economies, on the other hand, maintain relatively high average tariffs, with percentages often in the double-digit range. Although nations usually try to justify tariffs by appealing to the national interest, economists argue that tariffs generally aid some special interest group, but leave the world as a whole poorer.

The Effects of an Import Tariff in a Small Nation

A tariff imposed by a small nation will have no effect on prices in world markets. Just as one consumer cannot affect the price of pencils or automobiles by buying more or less, one small nation cannot affect the price of a good it imports from the rest of the world by changing it consumption. For a small nation a tariff will raise the price of imports to domestic consumers by the amount of the tariff. This will shift purchases to domestic sources, driving their price up until it reaches the new higher price of imports. The tariff increases the price of both the imported good and its domestically produced substitute. Although domestic producers will gain from higher prices, there will be net losses for two reasons. First, domestic consumers will be buying some goods from domestic producers that could be supplied from abroad more cheaply. Second, consumers will buy fewer units of the good so the gains consumers previously received on these units will no longer occur. These net losses can be better described graphically.

The S_X curve in Figure 5.1 is the supply of good X from domestic producers. The D_X curve in Fig. 5.1 is the demand for good X by domestic consumers. In the absence of trade, the price is $25, which is where quantity supplied equals quantity demanded.

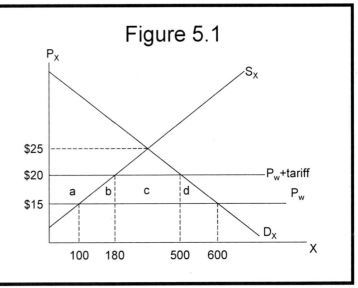

If the nation can buy good X at a world price of $15, shown as the flat line in Fig 5.1 at $15 (also labeled P_w), then the consumers of this nation will want to buy 600 units of good X while producers will want to produce 100 units of good X. The domestic excess demand at $15 is fulfilled by imports equal to 500 units.

If, now, a tariff of $5 per unit is imposed on imports of good X, then the new price faced by domestic consumers is $20. With the small nation assumption, the world price of $15 is unchanged because the nation is too small to affect world prices. Thus, the world price remains at $15, so that after the tariff of $5 is added, the relevant price of X in the nation is now $20.

With an increase in price from $15 to $20, producers increase production by 80 more units, for a total of 180 units supplied domestically. Consumers respond to the $20 price by buying 500 units. Now the amount imported is 320 units. The quantity imported falls as a result of the imposition of the tariff because domestic production has increased and the quantity demanded by domestic consumers has decreased. The government of the above nation will collect revenues from the tariff. With a quantity imported of 320 and a tariff of $5 per unit, the revenues from the tariff are $1600 and equal to area c in Fig. 5.1. Summarizing the effects of the tariff for the above case:

Consumption effect of a tariff = decrease in domestic units consumed = 100
Production effect of a tariff = increase in domestic units produced = 80
Trade effect of a tariff = decrease in units imported = 180
Revenue effect of a tariff = revenues produce by the tariff = $1600.

The cost of the tariff is the higher price that must be paid by consumers. The loss to consumers is represented by the loss of consumer surplus, which is the area *a+b+c+d*, in Fig. 5.1.

The benefit of the tariff is the gain in producer surplus plus the increased government revenues. The gain in producer surplus is indicated by area *a* in Fig. 5.1. The gain in revenues is area *c*, as explained previously. Essentially, consumers have lost *a+b+c+d*, of which area *a* has been redistributed to producers and area *c* has been redistributed to the government. The net result is a net loss equal to areas *b+d*. Area *b* represents the extra cost to consumers from buying domestically. Area *d* represents the consumer surplus that no longer is realized because units between 500 and 600 are no longer purchased. The losses represented by the area *b+d* is called the **deadweight loss** of the tariff because the area is not transferred anywhere; it no longer exists.

The Effects of an Import Tariff in a Large Nation

In a small nation, the domestic price of the good increases by the full amount of the import tariff, so the tariff is completely shifted to domestic consumers.

For a large country the tariff reduces domestic consumption of the good and, because the country is large, this reduced demand causes world prices to drop. As a result of the tariff, domestic consumers will still pay more, but the price increase to domestic consumers is less than the size of the tariff because the tariff is added to the world price, which has fallen. Part of the tariff has been shifted to foreign sellers of the good because the price falls on the world market. This is shown in Figure 5.2. The tariff is assumed to lower the world price from $15 to $13, so consumers pay $3 of the $5 because consumers now pay $18 rather than $15. Foreign producers pay $2 of the $5 tariff because the world price has fallen from $15 to $13.

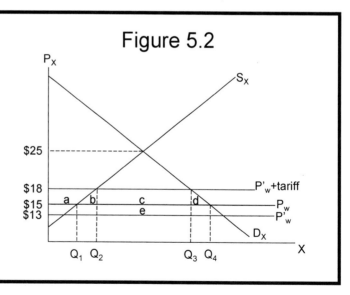

The gains and losses are now:

Loss of consumer surplus = area $a+b+c+d$
Gain in producer surplus = a
Gain in tariff revenues = $c+e$.

The gains minus the losses are $(a+c+e) - (a+b+c+d) = e - (b+d)$. If area e exceeds area $b+d$ then there is a gain to the nation imposing the tariff. If area e is less than area $b+d$, then there is a loss to the nation imposing the tariff. In the case of a large nation, a tariff can be beneficial, but is not necessarily so.

Not all tariffs will increase the welfare of a large nation. In the extreme, suppose a tariff is imposed that prohibits all imports. This is called a **prohibitive tariff**. A prohibitive tariff cannot be welfare enhancing because no part of the tariff can be shifted to foreigners – there is no e. Thus, the tariff must be of the right size to improve the welfare of a large nation. The tariff that maximizes the welfare of a large nation is called the **optimum tariff** and is somewhere between zero and the prohibitive tariff.

From a world perspective, however, a tariff never increases the total gains from trade. A tariff misallocates resources by increasing production in nations that do not have a comparative advantage thereby lowering world production. Although a large nation may gain from the tariff, its trading partners must necessarily lose more than the large nation gains.

The Effective Rate of Protection

Tariffs are generally intended to protect domestic industry from foreign competition but the degree to which they do so is often misestimated. If, for example, autos sell for $20,000 and use $15,000 of imported inputs, then there will be $5,000 of domestic activity that goes to produce the automobile. This is called **domestic value added**. If there is a tariff of 10% placed on automobiles, then the **nominal tariff** is 10%, but the **rate of effective protection** is quite different. Auto prices will increase to $22,000, which now makes domestic valued added equal to $7,000, which is a 40% increase over the original domestic value added. This increase in domestic value added is the rate of effective protection.

The rate of effective protection in an industry may also be negative. If a tariff is imposed on, say, steel to protect the steel industry, then protection to the auto industry will decrease. The higher cost of inputs means that for a given price of steel, the domestic valued added will drop. For most goods tariffs are cascaded, meaning that tariffs on the final produce are high relative to tariffs on inputs, in order to expand domestic value added. From an economic viewpoint, however, such protection reduces the welfare of a small nation due to the deadweight losses. For a large nation tariffs may increase the welfare of the large nation, but will misallocate resources and reduce world welfare.

Key Terms used in Chapter Summary and Review
(The list below is not necessarily the same as the list provided by the Salvatore text.)

Consumption effect of a tariff

Deadweight loss

Domestic value added

Nominal tariff

Optimum tariff

Production effect of a tariff

Prohibitive tariff

Revenue effect of a tariff

Tariffs

Trade effect of a tariff

Rate of effective protection

Multiple Choice Questions

1. If a tariff is imposed on an imported good by a small nation, which of the following will occur?
a) The price of the imported good and the domestic competing good will both increase.
b) The quantity consumed by domestic consumers will increase.
c) Domestic consumers will gain.
d) The nation will gain.

2. If a prohibitive tariff is imposed on imports of automobiles, then
a) Imports will be zero.
b) Consumer surplus will be zero.
c) Domestic production will fall to zero.
d) Domestic consumption will fall to zero.

3. If the consumption effect of a tariff were 50 units and the production effect of a tariff were 40 units, then imports would
a) Increase by 10 units.
b) Increase by 90 units.
c) Decrease by 90 units.
d) Decrease by 10 units.

4. If a tariff in a small country produces a deadweight loss of $60, reduces consumer surplus by $200, and increases producer surplus by $40, which of the following is correct?
a) National welfare falls by $220.
b) National welfare falls by $160.
c) Tariff revenues equal $100.
d) The price of the imported good must have fallen.

5. Which of the following must be true if a large nation imposes a tariff on an imported good?
a) The price received by domestic producers will fall.
b) The price received by foreign producers will fall.
c) Domestic consumers will gain.
d) The nation will gain.

6. A large nation imposes a tariff on an imported good, which causes the world price to fall by $4. At the new world price the large nation has deadweight losses of $500 and imports of 300. Which of the following must be true?
a) The large nation has gained.
b) Domestic producer surplus has fallen.
c) Domestic consumer surplus has increased.
d) Total tariff revenues must be less than the deadweight loss.

7. If a tariff of $10 per unit reduces the world price by $4, then
a) The nation imposing the tariff must be a small nation.
b) Domestic consumers pay $6 of the $10 per unit tariff.
c) Foreign producers pay $6 per unit of the $10 per unit tariff.
d) The nation imposing the tariff must necessarily lose.

8. Given that the imposition of a tariff will improve the welfare of a large nation, which of the following is true?
a) World welfare will increase if all large nations impose the tariff.
b) The large nation's gains are equal to its trading partners' losses.
c) World welfare will fall.
d) Large nations should impose a prohibitive tariff.

9. If a nation imposes a tariff on steel, an important input in the production of automobiles then
a) The nominal tariff on automobiles will increase.
b) The rate of effective protection on steel will decrease.
c) The rate of effective protection on automobiles will decrease.
d) Employment in the auto industry will increase.

10. If a nation imposes an import tariff of 20% on a final good that uses imported inputs, then
a) The effective rate of protection will be 20%.
b) The effective rate of protection will be greater than 20%.
c) The nominal rate of protection will be less than 20%
d) The nominal rate of protection will equal the effective rate of protection.

Problems and Discussion Questions

1. Figure 5.3 shows the effect of an import tariff. Answer the following based on Figure 5.3.
a) Is the demand curve in Figure 5.3, the demand by domestics, or the demand for domestic products?

b) What is the dollar amount of the tariff per unit?

c) Is the nation depicted in Figure 5.3 a small nation or a large nation?

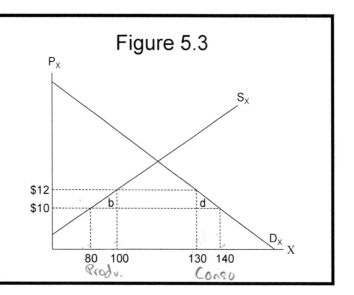

Figure 5.3

d) After all adjustments, what happens to the price of domestic production of good X as a result of the import tariff?

2. Using the numbers given in Figure 5.3, indicate the size of each of the following.
a) Consumption effect of the tariff.

b) Production effect of the tariff.

c) Trade effect of the tariff.

d) Revenue effect of the tariff.

3. Use Figure 5.3 to answer the following.
a) What is the dollar value of the welfare cost of the tariff to consumers?

b) What is the dollar value of the welfare benefit of the tariff to producers?

c) What is the dollar value of the tariff revenues?

d) Compare total benefits of the tariff to the costs to consumers and determine the dollar value of net losses from the tariff. Identify the net losses graphically in Fig. 5.3.

e) Calculate the area of triangles b and d in Fig. 5.3.

4. Table 1 gives the effect of a tariff on cotton sweaters. (Assume there is no difference between domestically produced sweaters and foreign produced sweaters.)

Table 1

	Free Trade	With a $4.00 Tariff
World Price of sweaters	$42.00	$42.00
Tariff per sweater	0	$4.00
Domestic Price of sweaters	$42.00	$46.00
Sweaters consumed domestically (million sweaters/year)	60	52
Sweaters produced domestically (million sweaters/year)	12	18
Sweaters imported (million packs/year	48	34

a) Using an upward sloping domestic supply curve and a downward sloping demand curve, calculate the losses to domestic consumers from the tariff.

b) Calculate the net effect on the country's welfare as a result of the tariff.

c) Based on the information given in Table 1, would the optimum import tariff on sweaters be negative, zero, or positive? Why?

5. Laptop computers are produced domestically and imported. The price of laptop computers is $1000 and domestic producers use $600 of imported inputs per laptop computer produced. What is the rate of effective protection if a 20% tariff is imposed on imports of laptop computers? Assume the nation is small.

6. As in Question 5, the price of laptop computers is $1,000 in a small nation, and laptops are both produced domestically and imported. If domestic producers use $600 worth of imported inputs, what is the effective rate of protection if a 20% tax is imposed on imported inputs?

Chapter 6
Nontariff Trade Barriers and the Political Economy of Protectionism

Chapter Outline

Chapter Summary and Review

Quotas

An **import quota** is a limit on the quantity of imports permitted into a country. Figure 6.1 shows a nation's domestic demand and supply for product Z. At the world price of P_w, free trade leads to imports of 50.

If the nation imposes an import quota of 32, then at the world price of P_w there will be an excess demand for goods. The total quantity demanded is 60 units. Of that demand for 60, 10 is satisfied by domestic producers, but only 32 units can be imported under the quota, so the total number of units supplied is 42. The excess demand will cause the price to increase, which will eliminate the shortage. As the price increases, domestic producers will

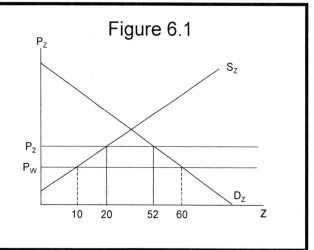

Figure 6.1

increase quantity supplied and domestic consumers will reduce quantity demanded. The price will increase to P_2, at which quantity demanded is 52, 20 of which is satisfied by domestic production and 32 is satisfied by the allowed imports of 32.

A quota that raises the price from P_W to P_2 has the same effects on production, consumption, and trade as a tariff that also raises the price from P_W to P_2. A quota, however, differs from a tariff in some important ways.

Tariffs directly produce revenues for government, while the revenue effect of a quota depends on the allocation of quota "rights" or licenses. Because a quota creates a price above the world price, the importers who can acquire licenses to import will reap monopoly profits. If government auctions off the import licenses, then the revenues will be identical to that of tariffs. If, however, import licenses are distributed by government officials in some other way (e.g. first-come, first-served), then those monopoly profits will be distributed in some way between government officials (bribes) and firms.

Quotas are also inflexible relative to tariffs. In growing economies, normal goods experience increases in demand through time. In the presence of a tariff this increased demand will be satisfied by imports at the world price. In the presence of a quota this increased demand will be satisfied by domestic production at an increasing price. Similarly, quotas protect domestic monopolies from foreign competition. Thus, import-competing firms will tend to prefer and lobby for import quotas over import tariffs.

Similar to quotas are **voluntary export restraints (VERs)**. A VER is an agreement initiated by an importing nation whereby an exporting nation agrees to reduce its exports. An example of a VER would be Japan agreeing to limit the exports of autos to the US at the bequest of the US. Like a tariff or a quota on automobiles, the purpose of the VER is to protect the auto industry. Although a quota and a VER are quantity limits established to protect domestic industry, there are some differences. First, voluntary export restraints invite the cooperation of foreign nations and so are less likely to invite retaliation as tariffs and quotas might. In addition, because the foreign nation allocates the license to its producers, the equivalent of tariff revenues or auctioned quota revenues are appropriated abroad. Whether those revenues are earned by the foreign government or foreign producers depends upon how the export licenses are allocated. Finally, VERs are negotiated with one other country, so the protection produced by a VER may erode as other nation attempt to fill the excess demand in the importing nation created by the VER.

Government regulations can act like quotas when they restrict imports of products not meeting local regulations. Safety and health regulations are particularly troublesome because although they may be motivated by genuine social concerns, they do protect local producers and will be supported by special interest groups. Disentangling the special interest group from the genuine need for some regulations can be very difficult. International trade is also affected by **government procurement policies**. Such policies require government agencies to give preference, up to some stated price percentage, to domestic suppliers. Although this acts like a tariff in raising the price paid for imports, it generates extra revenues to domestic suppliers like a quota.

Dumping

Dumping is defined as the export of a good at a price below cost, or at price below what the product is sold at in the producing nation. It is useful to classify dumping according to its frequency and intent.

Sporadic dumping is the occasional export of goods at prices lower than home prices (or costs). Sporadic dumping is most likely due to overestimates of potential sales in foreign markets. Once goods are shipped, it is often more profitable to liquidate inventories in foreign warehouses by lowering the price than by shipping the goods back to the home market. Sporadic dumping does not represent intent to do harm in foreign markets, and is no more harmful to producers in foreign countries than inventory sales by their domestic competitors.

Persistent dumping is international price discrimination in which a good is sold in a foreign market at a price lower than in the home market. An example is the sale of Japanese stereo equipment in the US market at price lower than what consumers in Japan pay for the same equipment.

Price discrimination occurs when the price elasticity of demand differs in different markets. Whenever the price elasticity of demand differs in two markets, and reselling cannot occur, then different prices can be charged in the two markets, with the higher price in the market with the lower price elasticity of demand. There are many examples of price discrimination. At state universities, state residents are usually charged lower tuition than out-of-state residents. Phone calls made during the day are more expensive than the same call made at night. Children pay less than adults at movie theatres. The basic purpose of price discrimination is to charge the price in each market that maximizes profits. The intent of persistent dumping is not to drive out competitors and then raise the price. If the demand conditions persist, the low price will persist.

Predatory dumping is the temporary export of a good at a lower price in order to drive out foreign producers in their home market, with the intent of then raising prices once competition is diminished. In order for predatory dumping to occur, a number of unlikely conditions have to be present. First, it must be assumed that once competitors are driven out of the market, some barrier prohibits their return. Next, it has to be cheaper for the predator to incur losses while driving out competitors than to simply buy their competitors at a fair price. Finally, it has to be assumed that foreign producers can withstand greater losses than competitors. If predatory dumping is such a good idea, then domestic producers could also incur losses and drive out other competitors, including foreign producers.

Whatever the form of dumping it should also be recognized that dumping can be beneficial to a nation's consumers. If foreign firms choose to export at a price lower than in their own market and others' markets, or at a price lower than it costs them to produce the product, then consumers will gain.

A form of dumping is also created by **export subsidies**. An export subsidy is a payment by government to an export firm that increases as the firm increases the quantity exported. Although current agreements between nations have illegalized export subsidies, there are other policies that achieve the same purpose. Examples include price floors for agricultural products which create domestic excess supply, and low interest loans for foreign countries firms to buy domestic exports. In the US the Export-Import Bank promotes US exports by providing loans with lower than market interest rates to foreign nations to buy US exports.

Because an export subsidy, of whatever form, provides an extra payment for export, domestic firms are receiving a higher price if they export. This will force domestic prices up because firms will choose to sell abroad, which will increase the domestic price until it equals the foreign price plus subsidy. This higher price increases the total amount sold by domestic firms (the intent of the subsidy), and reduces the amount consumed domestically, leaving a greater amount to be exported.

Although domestic producers gain by the higher price, part of that gain comes directly from consumers facing the higher price. In addition, taxpayers fund the gains by producers. The net result is a deadweight or efficiency loss to the nation subsidizing the exports. The actual price at which goods are being sold equals the world price; domestic producers receive a higher price only because of the subsidy. The cost of the additional goods sold by domestic producers is not justified by the world price. In addition, some goods are diverted away from domestic consumption that was previously beneficial to both domestic producers and consumers. In essence, a gift is given to foreign buyers in order for domestic producers to gain, but the net effect is negative because it misallocates resources. Domestic producers sell some goods abroad that foreign producers can produce more competitively.

Political Economy of Protectionism

Despite the economic arguments against import tariffs, import quotas, and other forms of protection, anti-trade sentiment continues to flourish. Some long-standing arguments against trade include the need to protect domestic labor from cheap foreign labor and a curiosity called the **scientific tariff**. The cheap foreign labor argument was addressed in Chapter 2. Essentially, competitiveness is not determined by the wage rate, but by the wage rate relative to productivity. It is true, however, as explained in Chapter 4, that trade will lower the return to the scarce factor in an economy, and that scarce factor may be labor. Nevertheless, there are still net gains from trade. The scientific tariff argument purports to "level the playing field" by imposing a tariffs that will equalize the price of domestic and foreign goods. This amounts to a policy of eliminating any trade, which would destroy the net gains from trade.

If the economic arguments for trade are indeed true, then why do governments continue protectionist policies and why do significant segments of the public think that domestic markets should be protected?

One compelling answer lies in the way that the gains and losses from trade are distributed. Trade produces gains for some and losses for others, with positive net gains. The lowering of tariffs, for example, hurts domestic producers, so domestic producers have a stake in maintaining trade barriers. On the other hand, consumers gain from cheaper imports, and gain more than producers lose, so on that basis we should hear more voices favoring trade because there are more consumers than producers. However, because there are many more consumers than producers, the gains from trade are divided over many consumers while the losses are divided over few producers. Thus, each consumer has some small gain from trade, and may not even be aware of the gains they receive from trade. How many consumers know that their automobile, domestic (made with foreign parts) or foreign, is considerably cheaper and better made because of imports? Producers, on the other hand, each bear a considerable cost from trade, even though all the costs for all producers are less than all the gains for all the consumers. In addition, it is more likely that producers will be aware that trade has produced the losses for they visibly compete with imports as part of their daily business.

The result is that consumers will have little incentive to organize and lobby for free trade, although it is in their interest, while producers will have considerable incentive to organize and lobby for protection.

There are some arguments for protection that may have some merit. One of these is the **infant industry argument**. The argument is that protection is necessary for a domestic industry to develop a true comparative advantage. Once a comparative advantage is gained, then a tariff (or another form of protection) will be no longer be necessary and the permanent gains to the industry will compensate for the temporary losses to consumers caused by the tariff.

The infant industry argument is subject, however, to a number of qualifications. Any argument for protection, reasonable on other grounds or not, is that it cannot be assumed that foreign nations will passively accept sanctions against its products. Foreign **retaliation** is always a real possibility, for which there are many historical examples. An additional consideration is the possibility that many industries will claim infant status and seek protection from foreign competitors, whether the case is valid or not.

To the degree that the infant industry argument is valid, it is an argument for a subsidy to the industry rather than a protectionist policy aimed at restricting imports. With a subsidy there is still a loss due to high-cost domestic production that replaces low-cost foreign production, as with a tariff, but subsides do not increase the price to consumers like tariffs do.

Another valid argument for protection is the optimum tariff argument discussed in the previous chapter. There is still, however, the threat of foreign retaliation, and an optimum tariff is not optimal from a global perspective because it misallocates resources. The gains by the nation imposing the optimum tariff are exceeded by the losses of trading partners.

Outsourcing and **offshoring** have received considerable recent attention in the popular press. Outsourcing and offshoring occur when inputs are produced abroad, either in, respectively, foreign factories or domestically owned factories located abroad. The basis for outsourcing and offshoring is simply comparative advantage and so produces net gains to both nations involved. Both activities, however, have produced negative reactions and calls for protection because, in part, of their visibility and the perception that they contribute to a significant loss of jobs.

Industrial policy and strategic trade policy, relatively recent arguments, establish possible gains from protectionism. For industries with significant external economies (see Chapter 5) government intervention (industrial policy) can establish a comparative advantage. Note from Chapter 5, though, that when there are external economies, the development of a comparative advantage in one industry means other nations will develop a comparative advantage in other industries. These arguments are politically popular and are internally consistent, but still assume that governments can pick winners and that foreign nations will not retaliate.

Key Terms used in Chapter Summary and Review
(The list below is not necessarily the same as the list provided by the Salvatore text.)

Export subsidies

Government regulations

Government procurement policies

Import quota

Industrial policy

Infant industry argument

Predatory dumping

Outsourcing

Offshoring

Persistent dumping

Retaliation

Scientific tariff

Sporadic dumping

Strategic trade policy

Voluntary export restraint (VER)

Multiple Choice Questions

1. If a nation imposes a quota and the licenses to import are auctioned off to domestic importers then:
a) The revenue effect of the quota and a tariff will be identical.
b) The purpose of the quota is defeated.
c) The quota will produce losses to import-competing firms.
d) The consumption effects of a quota and tariff will differ.

2. If import-competing firms expect the demand by domestic consumers for their product to increase they would prefer:
a) Free trade.
b) An import quota.
c) An import tariff.
d) A domestic tax on their production.

3. A quota raises the price of a good from $10 to $12. The quota restricts imports to 10,000 units and 1000 import licenses are printed. Each license allows the bearer to import 10 units. If the import licenses are auctioned, each license will be bid up to
a) $20.
b) $100.
c) $120.
d) $2,000.

4. Which of the following will occur if each nation imposes a scientific tariff on its imports?
a) Trade will occur on a fair basis.
b) Poor countries will gain more from trade.
c) No trade will occur.
d) Rich nations will dominate trade.

5. If the infant-industry argument is valid then which of the following is a better policy?
a) Subsidization of the infant industry.
b) An import tariff.
c) An import quota.
d) A VER.

6. Suppose US firms sell computers in the US market for a price of $700. Which of the following would qualify as dumping by Japan?
a) A Japanese firm sells computers in Japan and the US for $600.
b) A Japan firm sells computers in Japan for $650 and in the US for $625.
c) A Japanese firm sells computers in the US for $800.
d) A Japanese firm sells computers in Japan for $800.

7. A difference between an import quota of 300 and a VER of 300 is
a) The size of the production effect.
b) The size of the consumption effect.
c) The size of the import effect.
d) The nation that administers the quota.

8. Those who gain from trade do not lobby government for free trade while those who lose from trade tend to lobby for protection because
a) The gains are very widely distributed while the losses are concentrated.
b) The gains are small relative to losses.
c) Both the gains and losses are concentrated.
d) The gains are apparent while the losses are less obvious.

9. Predatory dumping is
a) Temporary.
b) Harmful to consumers.
c) Due to price discrimination.
d) Beneficial to domestic producers.

10. Suppose US consumers have a higher price elasticity of demand for French cheese than French consumers. Which of the following pricing structures is most likely?
a) The price of French cheese will be the same in the US and France.
b) The price of French cheese will be higher in France than in the US.
c) The price of French cheese will be lower in France than in the US.
d) US cheese will be cheaper than French cheese.

Problems and Discussion Questions

1. Figure 6.2 shows the domestic supply and demand for good X in a small country facing a world price of $7.00. An import quota of 4,000 units is imposed.

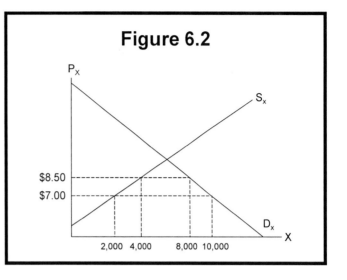

Figure 6.2

a) To enforce the quota, import licenses are auctioned to importers. Each license allows the license owner to import 1 units of good X. Calculate what the cost of each license will be.

b) Calculate the total revenues that will be earned through the auction of import licenses.

c) Calculate the welfare cost of the quota to the importing country.

d) Instead of auctioning the quotas to domestic importing firms, the governments of foreign countries that export the good are asked to voluntarily restrict their exports to 4,000 units. Calculate the welfare cost of this VER to the importing country.

e) In part d, you should have found that the welfare cost of a VER exceeds that of a simple quota. Why, then, would a country consider a VER for protection rather than a quota?

f) Based on Fig. 6.1 what is the dollar tariff per unit that will produce the same production and consumption effects as an import quota of 4,000 units?

2. US manufacturers have charged a number of Asian firms with dumping computer add-on equipment in the US market. Upon further investigation, it is established that the equipment is indeed being sold in the US market at a price lower than that charged in the foreign manufacturers' own market.
a) Is this dumping necessarily intended to inflict harm on the US?

b) Does this dumping necessarily harm the United States?

3. US manufacturers of computer hardware have charged a number of Asian firms with dumping computer add-on equipment in the US market. The US manufacturers present convincing evidence that the price of Asian equipment is lower than the price of equivalent US produced equipment. Would you construe this as dumping?

4. Explain why the textile and auto industries in the US have a history of high protection?

5. Why have nontariff barriers increased in importance relative to tariffs since WWII?

Chapter 7
Economic Integration

Chapter Outline

Chapter Summary and Review

The **European Free Trade Association** (EFTA), **North American Free Trade Agreement** (NAFTA), **European Union** (EU), **Central American Common Market** (CACM), **Latin American Free Trade Association** (LAFTA), **Southern Common Market** (Mercosur), **Free Trade of the Americas** (FTAA), and other similar organizations are examples of regional trading agreements. Regional trading agreements are forms of economic integration in which nations agree to reduce the economic barriers to the movement of products, labor, and capital. At the highest level of economic integration, nations also agree to coordinate monetary policy by adopting fixed exchange rates or, as in the case of Europe, a single currency. An example of complete economic unification is that of the fifty states that make up the United States.

In increasing order of integration, the most common forms of integration are **preferential trade arrangements**, **free trade areas**, **customs unions**, **common markets**, and **economic unions**.

Customs Union Theory

The analysis of trading agreements is normally conducted within the context of customs unions, but also applies to other forms of regional integration. A customs union is an agreement to adopt free trade between member nations of the customs union, and to erect a common tariff against the imports of non-member nations.

The purpose of a customs union is to take advantage of the gains from trade. Although it may appear that lowering tariffs and relaxing other barriers to trade are consistent with the gains described by the standard trade model, such arrangements may actually reduce national economic welfare.

The analysis of a customs union is very similar to that used to analyze tariffs in Chapter 5, but now there are two import prices to consider. Assume that prior to the formation of the customs union that a nation has a specific tariff applied to all imports, no matter what their source. (Recall from Chapter 5 that a specific tariff is a tariff of some dollars per unit, rather than a percentage.) Prior to the formation of a customs union a nation imposes a tariff on all of its trading partners. The formation of a customs union is an agreement with some trading partners to eliminate the tariff. Figure 7.1 is the demand and supply of a good in a nation, say Nation 1, which will enter into a customs union agreement with some of its trading partners. For simplicity assume only three nations: Nations 1, 2 and 3.

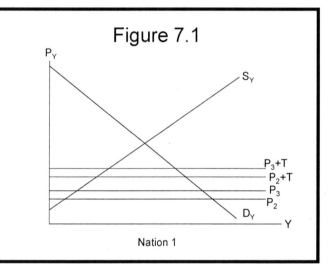

Suppose the price of imported products from Nation 2, P_2, is lower than the price of imported products from Nation 3, P_3, as shown in Fig. 7.1. With the tariff both prices will be higher, as is shown in Fig. 7.1. As a result, ***prior to the formation of the customs union, Nation1 will import product Y only from Nation 2***. If Nation 1 and Nation 2 form a customs union, then the relevant prices faced by Nation 1 are P_3+T and P_2. Nation 3 is not part of the customs union so a tariff will still be applied to Nation 3. Nation 1 will continue to import Y from Nation 2. The customs union has lowered the price of imports by the amount of the tariff. In Chapter 5, a tariff in a small nation was seen to produce deadweight losses, which means that eliminating a tariff will produce gains equal to the deadweight losses. The customs union where a trading partner's prices are as described in Fig. 7.1 amounts to an elimination of a tariff on a trading partner, so this customs union will increase the economic welfare of Nation 1. This is an efficient organization because goods are being produced where they are the cheapest. This is an example of **trade creation** from a customs union because the tariff reduction increases Nation 1's imports from Nation 2. Trade creating customs unions are welfare enhancing. In general, if a group of nations are already trading with another, then a customs union will promote the welfare of those nations.

Now suppose a different situation. Suppose Nations 1 and 2 establish a customs union, and Nation 2's prices are initially above Nation 3's prices, as shown in Figure 7.2. The prices of P_2 and P_3 represent the opportunity cost of production, so P_3 is the low-cost producer of Y.

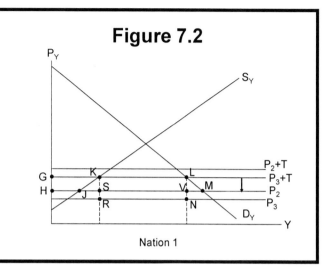

Prior to the customs union Nation 1 will import from Nation 3 at a price of P_3+T. When Nation 1 and 2 from the customs union, P_2+T will drop to P_2, but Nation 3's prices will remain at P_3+T. Now Nation 1 will import from Nation 2 rather than from Nation 3. Now it is not clear if the customs union improves the welfare of Nation 1. Nation 1 does face lower prices for imports (falling from P_3+T to P_2 –see arrow in Fig. 7.2), so trade does expand, which is trade creating and welfare enhancing. Nation 1, however, now imports from the high-cost producer. **Trade diversion** occurs in that trade is diverted from the low-cost producer, which reduces welfare. The price decreases from P_3+T to P_2, an amount that is less than the tariff. Some lost revenues from eliminating the tariff are not recovered because the price falls less than the tariff.

Using the labeled points in Fig. 7.2, the gains and losses, as well as net changes, to Nation1 from the customs union between Nations 1 and 2 are listed below. (The series of letters refer to areas in Fig. 7.2)

Gain in Consumer Surplus = GLMH
Lost Producer Surplus = HJKG
Lost Tariff Revenue = RKLN

Using the above areas:

Gains – Losses = GLMH – HJKG - RKLN KSJ+LVM – SRNV.

The triangles KSJ and LVM represent the gains from trade creation while the rectangle SRNV represents the loss from trade diversion. The welfare effect of a customs union depends upon the sizes of the two triangles relative to the rectangle.

Trade creation and trade diversion are concepts produced by a *static* analysis of customs unions — an analysis of the allocation of existing resources. Customs unions also provide other potentially important static gains. First, a relaxation of trade restrictions will lower administrative costs associated with collecting border taxes, policing borders, etc. Next, an economic agreement among a number of countries will increase both economic and political power. Negotiating with the EU is clearly quite different than negotiating with one member of the EU. This increased political power can produce significant gains to members of the customs union, and the increased economic power can have important terms of trade effects. Each member of a customs union is unlikely to have the economic power necessary to change its terms of trade with the rest of the world through imposing the optimum tariff (see Chapter 5). A customs union, however, is likely to have some economic power and be able to use tariffs to produce a favorable change in its terms of trade.

There are also potential dynamic gains from customs unions. These are identical to the dynamic gains from freer trade in general and include *increased competition, economies of large-scale production, stimulus to investment, and the gains from increased mobility of labor and capital.*

Key Terms used in Chapter Summary and Review
(The list below is not necessarily the same as the list provided by the Salvatore text.)

Central American Common Market
  (CACM)
Common markets
Customs unions
Economic unions
European Free Trade Association
  (EFTA)
European Union (EU)
Free trade areas

Free Trade of the Americas (FTAA)
Latin American Free Trade Association
  (LAFTA)
North American Free Trade Agreement
  (NAFTA)
Preferential trade arrangements
Southern Common Market (Mercosur)
Trade creation
Trade diversion

Multiple Choice Questions

1. A customs union is an agreement to remove barriers to trade among its members and to:
a) Adopt the same currency.
b) Adopt a fixed exchange rate.
c) Adopt a common external tariff.
d) Leave each nation determine its own tariff policy.

2. If Nation B is the source of all of Nation A's imports, then a customs union between Nations A and B will:
a) Be trade creating.
b) Be trade diverting.
c) Be both trade creating and diverting, but the trade diversion effect will be larger.
d) Not affect trade between A and B.

3. The trade diversion effect is due to:
a) Identical prices among all trading partners.
b) The tariff exceeding the reduction in price.
c) The deadweight losses.
d) Lost consumer surplus.

4. Which of the following will occur in Nation 1 if it joins a customs union?
a) Welfare will necessarily increase.
b) Both consumer and producer surplus will increase.
c) Both consumer and producer surplus will decrease.
d) Consumer surplus will increase more than producer surplus decreases.

5. Nation 1 imports bicycles from Nations 2 and 3. If the prices of bicycles imported from Nation 2 and 3 are the same then for Nation 1 a customs union with Nation 2 will
a) Be unnecessary.
b) Be trade diverting.
c) Be trade creating.
d) Have no effect on Nation 1's welfare.

6. A nation imposes a specific tariff of $10 on its imports. A customs union leads to a decrease in the price of imported goods by $4. The customs union is
a) Trade creating only.
b) Trade diverting only.
c) Both trade creating and trade diverting.
d) Welfare reducing.

7. Nation 1 currently imports gloves from Nation 2 at a price of $12. Nation 1 and Nation 3 enter into a customs union, after which the price of the same gloves from Nation 3 is $14. The customs union is
a) Trade diverting.
b) Trade creating.
c) Neither trade creating nor trade diverting.
d) Both trade diverting and trade creating.

8. A dynamic effect of customs unions is
a) Trade creation.
b) Economies of large-scale production.
c) Less mobility of labor.
d) Coordinated monetary policy.

9. The gains from trade creation are due to
a) The elimination of deadweight losses.
b) The loss of tariff revenues.
c) Product differentiation.
d) Reduced producer surplus.

10. A possible welfare reducing effect of a customs union is
a) The change in deadweight losses.
b) Reduced administrative expenses.
c) Increased trade.
d) The loss of tariff revenues.

Problems and Discussion Questions

1. Why does a regional trading agreement between Canada, the United States, and Mexico make more economic sense than one between Burma, Tanzania and the United States?

2. How might a customs union lead to
a) Economies of large-scale production?

b) Gains from increased competition?

c) Greater investment in the customs union?

3. Other than trade diversion, what is a possible threat to free trade created by the formation of customs unions?

4. Figure 7.1 shows an importing country before the formation of a customs union. S_n represents the supply from future non-members, S_m represents the supply from future members, and T is the tariff. Assume that after the formation of the customs union, T is maintained against non-members and eliminated for members. Where necessary, use letters from Fig. 7.1 to answer the following questions.

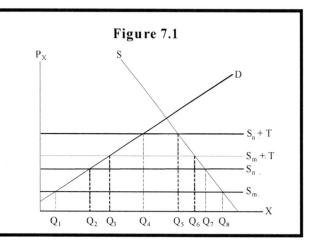

Figure 7.1

a) What is the level of domestic production, domestic consumption, and imports prior to the formation of the customs union? From which nation will these imports be purchased?

b) What is the level of domestic production, domestic consumption, and imports after the formation of the customs union? From which nation will these imports be purchased?

c) Will the customs union be trade diverting or trade creating? Explain.

d) Will there necessarily be gains from the formation of such a customs union?

5. Answer the same questions posed in Question 2, but use Figure 7.2 for the source of your answers.

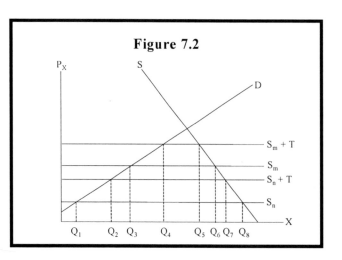

Figure 7.2

6. Answer the same questions posed in Question 2, but use Figure 7.3 for the source of your answers.

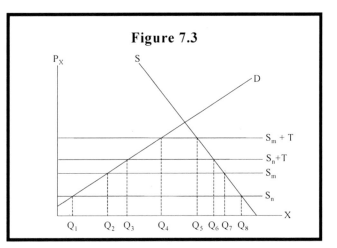

Figure 7.3

Chapter 8
Growth and Development with International Trade

Chapter Outline

Chapter Summary and Review

Growth and Development

A majority of the world's population lives in the developing world, characterized by, among other things, low per capita real GDP, poor health, high illiteracy, rapid population growth, and low growth of GDP. Growth in a nation's standard of living depends to a large part on increases in factor supplies. The nature of that growth depends upon the relative growth rates of the factor supplies.

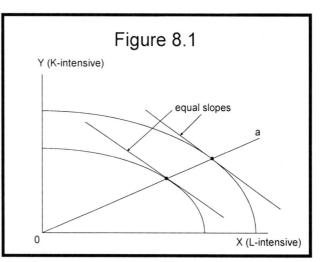

Figure 8.1

Assume for simplicity that the only two factors of production are capital and labor. **Balanced growth** occurs when both K and L grow at identical rates. If there are constant returns to scale (output grows at the same rate as the growth rates of each factor), then all absolute numbers are larger by the growth in the factors. If capital and labor double, then output will double. In the case of balanced growth, the production possibility frontier shifts out in a uniform fashion as shown in Figure 8.1. The slope of the ppfs along any ray from the origin, such as 0a, will be identical.

Balanced growth with constant returns to scale produces no change in per capita incomes. Output has doubled, but so has the number of people, assuming that a doubling of the labor force also means a doubling of population. This is true if the dependency ratio – ratio of non-working population to population in the labor force – remains constant.

If one factor increases faster than the other, then absolute numbers are larger but relative amounts, like per capita income, change. If the amount capital increases relative to the amount of labor, then the ppf will shift out because both goods use capital. If good Y is capital intensive and good X is labor intensive, then the vertical intercept in Fig. 8.1 will increase more than the horizontal intercept (this diagram is not shown). If capital grows faster than the labor force, then the productivity of labor will increase because each laborer, on average will have more capital with which to work. Higher productivity means each laborer produces more, so per capita income will increase.

If, on the other hand, the labor force increases relative to the capital stock, then the ppf will shift out more for the labor-intensive good. If labor grows faster than capital, then labor productivity will fall as each laborer has less capital with which to work. As labor productivity falls, per capita incomes fall.

Trade and Development
Although the purpose of trade theory is not to explicitly address growth and development questions, trade theory has made some important contributions to development issues. The traditional comparative advantage argument has been viewed as a static argument that promotes the status quo of poverty in developing nations. Because most developing nations are low-cost producers of primary products, the principle of comparative advantage is seen as keeping them as producers of primary products rather than fostering a transition to manufacturing and industrial production, which are taken as signs of progress. Trade, however, can promote genuine development as well as produce the static comparative advantage based gains.

In nations with ineffective fiscal and monetary policies, trade can provide increased employment through export markets. This is the **vent for surplus** argument. Surplus domestic production of minerals and agricultural goods can be sold in export markets. The increased production possible through expanded markets may also allow firms to reap the benefits of economies of scale should they exist. Perhaps equally important is the spread of ideas, technology, and finance that access and exposure to international markets may promote. Trade can also be instrumental in promoting competition in small markets that may be monopolized by a few local firms.

An important controversy in the debate over the role of trade in economic development is the effect of long-run changes in the terms of trade of developing nations. Generally speaking, the terms-of-trade is the price of exports relative to the price of imports. There are a number of specific measures of the terms of trade, the simplest of which is the **net barter, or commodity terms of trade**. The commodity terms of trade is expressed as an index, with the base year set equal to 100, and each subsequent year's terms of trade stated relative to 100. The barter terms of trade can be written as

$$N = (P_X/P_M)100.$$

N is the barter terms of trade, P_X is a price index of exports, and P_M is a price index of imports. Both P_X and P_M are set equal to 100 in the base year. If in the year following the base year the price of exports increases by 10% and the price of imports increase by 5%, then the new barter terms of trade will be

$$N = (110/105)100 = 104.8.$$

There has been an improvement in the barter terms of trade by 4.8% with the price received for exports increasing by more than the price paid for imports.

Another common measure of the terms of trade is the **income terms of trade.** The income terms of trade represents the quantity of imports that export earnings will buy. Export earnings are measured by P_X times Q_X, where Q_X is an index of the quantity of exports. Dividing the export earnings by the price of imports produces the income terms of trade, i.e.,

$$I = (P_X)(Q_X)/P_M = (P_X/P_M)Q_X,$$

where I is the income terms of trade.

The controversy over the terms of trade stems from the argument that the terms of trade of developing countries can be expected to fall over time, turning in favor of the developed nations. If true, then although trade may bring gains to both developing and developed nations, it is the developed nations that will continually secure a larger share of the gains from trade as prices move in their favor.

The basis for the argument that the terms of trade will deteriorate for developing nations is the nature of the labor markets in developed nations versus developing nations. In developing nations, labor is generally weak, marked by high rates of unemployment and nonexistent or weak labor unions and labor laws. If there are labor productivity increases, then the productivity gains will not be realized by weak labor in the form of higher wages. Rather, the cost savings due to increased productivity will be passed along in the form of lower prices. Thus, the price of the exports of developing nations (P_X) will decrease over time.

In developed nations, strong labor will appropriate the productivity gains in the form of higher wages, leaving prices faced by the developing nations (P_M) unaffected. Strong unions may even be able to increase wages faster than productivity, which forces the prices in developed nations to increase.

In addition, as incomes grow in the world, the demand for the manufactured goods of the developed nations will increase, causing the prices of manufactured goods to increase while little of the new income will go to the agricultural goods produced by developing nations. Simply stated, the income elasticity of demand for manufactured goods is higher than the income elasticity of demand for agricultural goods.

Empirical studies conducted to test this hypothesis are subject to statistical problems, but some interesting themes emerge. First, there seems to have been a small secular decline in the barter terms of trade, but an increase in the income terms of trade. That is, although the price of exports relative to imports for developing nations have declined, the ability to import has increased due to an even faster growth in export volumes. The income terms of trade may be more important to developing nations if the interest is in measuring what these nations can buy from the rest of the world with their export earnings.

If a nation's growth leads to excess supply of its export good on world markets, then the price of the export good will fall, causing deterioration in the terms of trade. If the terms of trade fall by enough to offset the additional output due to growth, then growth may actually cause a nation to be worse off. This phenomenon, called **immiserizing growth**, although possible is unlikely.

In addition to the *level* of the relative price of exports faced by developing nations, there is the separate concern of the *volatility* of export prices. If export prices exhibit volatility, then the economy that relies on those export earnings to finance domestic consumption and investment will also exhibit volatility.

As mentioned, many developing economies tend to export primary products like minerals and agricultural goods. Primary product prices exhibit relatively high volatility because of the price elasticities of demand and supply. The price elasticity of demand by developed nations for the primary product exports of developing nations is relatively low because such products make up a very small part of developed countries' incomes. When a small proportion of income is spent on a product, then a price change of the product is relatively meaningless, producing a small response. (Consider the effect of a change in the price of the daily newspaper for the average US family.) In addition, primary products may have few close substitutes, contributing to the low price elasticity of demand.

The price elasticity of supply for primary products is small because of the difficulty of increasing input use in developing countries in response to a price increase. In addition, the production of agricultural goods cannot be increased easily until the next growing season.

With low price elasticities on both the supply and demand sides, both the demand and supply curves will be steep. The consequence of shifts of demand or supply is a large change in price and a small change in quantity. (Draw steep but not perfectly vertical supply and demand curves and shift one of the curves.) Thus, when supply or demand curves shift there will be considerable movements in price.

In response to possible volatility of export prices, countries have pursued policies to stabilize such prices (marketing boards, buffer stocks, export controls, and purchase contracts), but the policies have generally not proven successful due to the cost of the policies themselves.

Although this **export instability** argument is valid, the evidence suggests that it does not extend to all products, and, in any case, the level of export instability is small and has not proven to significantly impede development.

Partially in response to the perceived problems associated with the production and export of primary products, and to the equating of industrialization with development, a number of developing countries in the 1950s, 1960s and 1970s pursued industrialization through **import-substitution industrialization (ISI)**. ISI is the use of tariffs to reduce imports of industrial products, and to promote and protect domestic industry in order to replace imports of industrial products. It is, indeed, easier to promote domestic industry by erecting import tariffs than it is to promote industrialization through exports by persuading other countries to lower their trade barriers. It is also clear that a domestic market exists for the industrial products because the goods are already imported. Foreign firms will also have an incentive to locate operations (**tariff factories**) in the domestic market of developing countries pursuing ISI in order to avoid the high tariffs that would be applied to their exports to those countries.

There are, however, distinct disadvantages to an ISI policy. First, the domestic market in most developing countries is limited, making economies of scale difficult to achieve. Second, as is the case with any form of protection, a special interest group is created that diverts attention from profiting through promoting efficiency to profiting by maintaining the trade barriers. Finally, ISI can get costly. Effort will initially be devoted to replacing the imports that are most easily produced domestically. In time, however, further expansion will require more technologically advanced production that is not so easily replicated domestically, unless the necessary capital is imported, which is exactly what the ISI policy tries to discourage.

The experience with ISI has, on balance, not been favorable. Very simply, ISI tries to promote the production of goods in which *other* nations have a comparative advantage, as demonstrated by the original trade pattern prior to the ISI policy. Moreover, the high tariffs necessary to protect inefficient industries produce significant costs to domestic consumers. ISI also copies foreign production methods, which for most less developed economies means capital-intensive production methods, producing only modest employment gains and over-investment in physical capital. Other sectors' investment needs are neglected, providing few jobs for labor displaced from the import-substitution sectors.

The alternative to ISI is **export-oriented industrialization**. The advantages of export-oriented industrialization are that it emphasizes a nation's comparative advantage and expansion and economies of scale are not limited by the size of the domestic market. The cost of such *outward-looking policies* is the effort needed to compete in the world market in addition to the trade barriers often imposed by developed countries on the labor-intensive goods of the developing countries. In response to the failure of ISI, a number of nations have pursued export-oriented industrialization beginning in the 1980s, supported by the World Bank and the new agreements negotiated in the Uruguay Round that reduced the trade barriers of the developed countries.

Key Terms used in Chapter Summary and Review
(The list below is not necessarily the same as the list provided by the Salvatore text.)

Balanced growth

Buffer stocks

Commodity terms of trade

Export controls

Export instability

Export-oriented industrialization

Immiserizing growth

Import-substitution industrialization (ISI)

Income terms of trade

Marketing boards

Net barter terms of trade

Purchase contracts

Tariff factories

Vent for surplus

Multiple Choice Questions

1. If there are constant returns to scale and capital and labor both double, then production per laborer
a) Will double.
b) Will decrease.
c) Will more than double.
d) Will be unchanged.

2. If the dependency ratio is unchanged, then growth in the labor force with no change in capital will
a) Reduce production.
b) Leave production unchanged.
c) Reduce per capita production.
d) Increase production per laborer.

3. Which of the following will occur if export prices double, export quantities halve and import prices remain unchanged?
a) The commodity terms of trade remain constant.
b) The net barter terms of trade remain constant.
c) The income terms of trade remain constant.
d) The income terms of trade increase.

4. Which of the following is a possible cause of a decrease in a nation's commodity terms of trade?
a) Low price elasticity of demand for the nation's export good.
b) High price elasticity of supply for the nation's export good.
c) Low income elasticity of demand for a nation's export good.
d) Low income elasticity of demand for a nation's import good.

5. Import-Substitution Industrialization a policy that promotes development by:
a) Stabilizing export prices.
b) Stabilizing import prices.
c) Promoting labor force growth.
d) Using import protection to promote domestic industry.

6. One reason why trade may promote development is that trade:
a) Stabilizes export prices of developing nations.
b) Promotes the spread of ideas.
c) Has increased the net barter terms of trade.
d) Has lowered the income terms of trade.

7. If world demand increases for a nation's export good then
a) The commodity terms of trade will increase.
b) The commodity terms of trade will be unchanged.
c) The income terms of trade will decrease.
d) The income terms of trade will be unchanged.

8. Export-oriented industrialization is generally preferred to import-substitution industrialization because it
a) Relies on an already existing domestic market.
b) Relies on the nation's comparative advantage.
c) Export prices are more volatile than import prices.
d) There is more competition in the import sector.

9. If the rate of growth of the capital stock exceeds the rate of growth of labor then
a) Wages will fall.
b) Capital-labor ratios will fall.
c) The productivity of labor will fall.
d) The amount produced per laborer will increase.

10. Which of the following could cause unstable export prices?
a) High income elasticity of demand for exports.
b) High price elasticity of supply and demand for exports.
c) Low price elasticity of supply and demand for exports.
d) Buffer stocks.

Problems and Discussion Questions

1. Match the graphs in Figure 8.2 with the changes described below. Assume that X is the capital-intensive good so Y is the labor-intensive good.
a) A 10% increase in supply of capital.

b) A 10% increase in the supply of labor.

c) A 10% increase in both the supply of capital and labor.

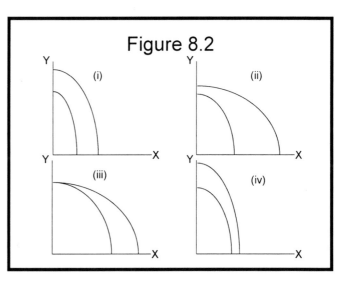

Figure 8.2

d) Technical progress in the production of Good X, but not Good Y.

e) Technical progress at the same rate in the production of both Goods X and Y.

2. For the changes described in question 1, explain the effect on total income and per capita incomes, assuming that the dependency ratio does not change.

3. The price indices of exports and imports, and a quantity index of exports are contained in Table 8.1 below for various years for the country of Mauritius.

Table 8.1

Year	Export Price Index	Import Price Index	Export Quantity Index
1992	108.7	102.1	100.0
1993	104.5	99.9	104.2
1994	107.4	105.3	105.1

Source: Adapted from the IMF's, International Financial Statistics, April 1997.

a) Calculate the commodity terms of trade of Mauritius for the years 1992-1994.

b) Comment on the meaning of the changes in the commodity terms of trade from 1992-1994.

c) Calculate the income terms of trade for the years 1992-1994. Set the 1992 income terms of trade equal to 100.

d) Comment on the meaning of the changes in the income terms of trade from 1992-1994.

4. a) What has been the long-run experience of countries that have pursued import-substitution industrialization?

b) What's a possible justification for the view that export-oriented industrialization is a better development strategy than import-substitution industrialization?

5. Comment on the following statement. "If the ppf shifts out and the terms of trade are unaffected, then a country is unambiguously better off because a higher community indifference curve can be reached."

6. a) Explain why primary goods can be expected to exhibit more price instability than manufactured goods.

b) How could buffer stocks be used to reduce this instability?

Chapter 9
International Resource Movements and Multinational Corporations

Chapter Outline

Chapter Summary and Review

In the Heckscher-Ohlin model, trade and the gains from trade stem from different factor endowments between nations. The economic incentive for the movement of labor and capital between nations is also due to different factor endowments and intensities.

In a world with few barriers to the movement of capital, capital would move from nations where capital is abundant and cheap to nations where capital is scarce and expensive. Owners of capital have an incentive to provide capital where they can receive the higher return. Similarly, labor would move from nations where labor is abundant and cheap to nations where labor is scarce and expensive. Labor, *ceteris paribus*, moves to where higher wages are earned.

The movement of capital and labor to, respectively, higher returns and wages produces gains because factors are used where they are more productive, the source of higher returns and wages. If capital and labor cannot or does not freely move, then labor and capital can achieve the higher returns and wages by exporting products containing their abundant, cheap factor. Over the past fifty years, both barriers to trade in products and barriers to the movement of factors of production have fallen, resulting in both expanded trade and movements of factors of production.

The international movement of capital includes **portfolio investment** and **direct investment**. International portfolio investment is the international exchange of financial

Chapter 9: International Resource Movements and Multinational Corporations

assets. If a US citizen or firm purchases bonds, stocks, bank accounts, etc. in another country, then international portfolio investment has occurred. Direct investment, on the other hand, implies not only the acquisition of foreign assets, but control as well. If a US firm opens a factory in Poland, then the US firm controls the factory and direct investment has occurred. Similarly, if a Dutch firm buys enough stock to have a controlling interest in a factory located in Milwaukee, then direct investment has occurred. What constitutes a controlling cannot be precisely determined. Clearly, anything above 50% ownership is a controlling interest, but significant control can be exercised with much smaller percentages. The usual rule-of-thumb is that control occurs with 10% ownership.

The basic motivation for portfolio investment is to diversify financial portfolios. A well-known principle of **risk diversification** is that combinations of assets will outperform single assets if the returns on the combinations of assets are not highly correlated.

In Figure 9.1, the returns on assets A and B are shown. Note that both assets average about 12%. It is assumed in Fig. 9.1 that when one asset's return increases, the other decreases. If you held only Asset A, then you would bear all of the fluctuations associated with asset A; likewise for holding only Asset B. If, however, you split your funds between assets A and B, then your total portfolio value would exhibit small fluctuations, but you would still earn the 12% average, as shown in bottom diagram in Fig 9.1. Diversification among assets whose returns are inversely related can produce lower risk for the same return.

Foreign assets are likely candidates for diversification because they do not move as closely with domestic assets as do domestic assets with other domestic assets because foreign and domestic assets are subject to different economic forces.

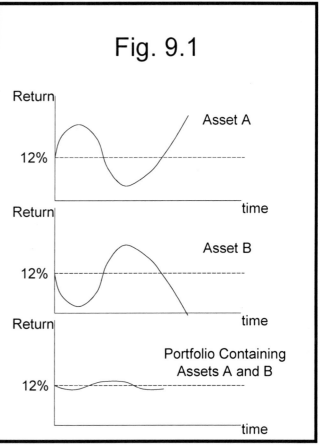

Fig. 9.1

In addition to movements of financial capital for diversification reasons, there is the movement of financial capital to take advantage of different interest rates. Government securities in Germany may offer higher interest rates for lenders in the US, while Japan may offer lower rates for US borrowers. In all of these cases an additional important concern is the change in the exchange rate over the term that foreign assets are held.

The motivation for direct foreign investment, like portfolio investment, also includes risk and return considerations. Foreign plants can be more productive and profitable because of more favorable tax treatment, less trade barriers, a better social infrastructure, access to cheaper inputs, etc. A firm may also wish to diversify its production facilities. Because the time path of profitability of foreign facilities may differ from domestic facilities, there may be diversification benefits as in the portfolio investment case.

If a firm has control over a unique input in its own production process, such as patents, managerial expertise, technical expertise, etc., it may decide not to sell the input to foreign markets, but undertake the actual production in foreign markets. By controlling the production process, control over the unique input is maintained, which does not allow others to easily develop a similar expertise. In this case the firm is expanding through **horizontal integration** — expanding by producing identical or similar products in other markets. The Salvatore text offers IBM as an example. IBM does not license foreign producers to produce IBM computers, but locates its own plants abroad in order to control patents, trade secrets, quality and service.

If a US firm acquires ownership of foreign firms that provide important inputs to the US firm, then the US firm is expanding through **vertical integration**. Vertical integration includes expanding by acquiring foreign firms that provide inputs earlier in the production process, or by providing inputs later in the production process, such as marketing and retail services. Steel firms may own and mine iron ore deposits in other countries rather than buying foreign iron ore from foreign-owned sources, and auto firms may own retail establishments in other countries, rather than selling autos to foreign-owned retailers.

International movements of both direct and portfolio capital finance real investment in other countries. Capital moves to where the return (or risk-adjusted return) on real investment is higher. This movement of capital produces a gain. If capital moves from low productivity uses to high productivity uses, then international production will increase. (In competitive markets, real returns and marginal productivity are equivalent.) There may be a distributional issue, but there is an improved allocation of resources because world production is higher. The distributional issue is that as capital flows out of the **home nation**, labor in the home country will have to find new jobs in the home country. In the **host country**, labor will gain from having access to foreign capital, and capital in the host country will lose as foreign capital drives down the rate of return in the host country.

Another consideration in the international movement of capital is the balance of payments effect. As capital flows out of a country, the balance of payments will move towards deficit, but this may be mitigated in the future as income on the foreign investment returns. In the case of direct investment, there may also be increased exports to supply the facilities located abroad. On the other hand, foreign facilities may mean that exports fall, as production for the foreign market is located in the foreign market rather than in the domestic market. There may even be increased imports if a substantial number of domestic production facilities shift abroad. Home nation consumption may be satisfied from relocated facilities that were originally located domestically.

Finally, the movement of capital may affect the tax base and tax collections in both source and host countries. Most countries agree to avoid double taxation, with the high-tax country collecting only the difference in tax rates. If the tax rate in the United States is 50%, and the foreign tax rate is 30%, then the United States will collect 20% on the profits of US foreign subsidiaries, while the foreign nation will collect 30%.

Direct foreign investment is undertaken primarily by **multinational corporations (MNC's)**, also known as **transnational corporations (TNC's)**. MNC's are firms that control or manage production in more than one nation. MNC's account for as much as one-fourth of world production. Shipments between the parent firm and foreign branches account for approximately one-third of global manufacturing trade.

MNC's have risen to exploit the competitive advantages associated with increasing the size of the firm. These advantages include the monopoly power that may come with horizontal integration, the control of inputs that comes with vertical integration, the ability to exploit economies of scale in distribution, production and information, and the flexibility to locate R&D, production and distribution facilities in the nations that are best suited for those activities. Size also brings significant bargaining power in both the economic and political spheres. Finally, because intra-firm shipments can be priced internally **(transfer pricing)**, MNC's can price inputs high (understating profits) when they are shipped to branches in high tax areas, and price final goods low (understating profits) when they are shipped from branches in high tax areas.

The rapid growth of MNC's since WWII has raised important issues concerning their effect on the world economy. From the home country's perspective, foreign investment is usually perceived as the exporting of jobs. However, if the motive for locating affiliates abroad is cheaper production costs, then it is conceivable that the jobs would have been lost anyway. Additionally, as foreign investment increases, the home office will expand, creating new administrative and financial service jobs in the home office.

There is also the issue of the diffusion of technology. By locating production facilities abroad, foreign nations become aware of new technology, possibly eroding the technological edge of the home country. On the other hand, expanded trade may spur even more R&D in the home country, advancing technological knowledge beyond what would exist in the absence of MNCs.

MNCs, as explained above, can also use transfer pricing to minimize home country tax payments, thereby eroding the tax base of the home country. The ability to locate abroad also allows MNC's to avoid regulations and policies in the home market, eroding the power of the national government to affect economic conditions.

Criticisms of MNCs from the host countries are more controversial. Many host countries are concerned about their dependency on foreign firms. Foreign firms use host country resources, influence host country tastes and culture, and bend host country policies, all to their own ends, which may not necessarily be in the perceived self-interest of the host country. In response many host countries have regulated foreign direct investment through tax rates and/or minimum local ownership rules.

Although labor migration can be motivated by social and political conditions, it appears that the economic incentives have become more important since World War II. If labor moves due to a perceived difference in real wages, then labor migration will produce economic gains. As labor leaves low wage areas for high wage areas, world income and production will increase by the differential.

Although labor migration increases world income, there are distributional issues, as in the case of international capital movements. A major concern is the effect on wages in the nation experiencing the influx of workers. In the United States, labor groups are generally opposed to immigration because immigration increases the supply of labor, driving down local wage rates, until they are roughly equal to foreign wage rates. Labor in the supplying country, on the other hand will support out-migration because it allows its population to seek higher wages, and raises the wages of labor remaining in the supplying country. This sentiment in the supplying country only applies for unskilled labor. In the case of skilled labor, migration out of the country is seen as a loss of valuable human capital, known as **brain drain**. This does indeed represent a cost to the supplying country that has expended valuable resources in training and educating skilled workers.

Key Terms used in Chapter Summary and Review
(The list below is not necessarily the same as the list provided by the Salvatore text.)

Brain drain

Direct investment

Home nation

Horizontal integration

Host nation

Multinational corporations (MNC's)

Portfolio investment

Risk diversification

Transnational corporations (TNC's)

Transfer pricing

Vertical integration

Multiple Choice Questions

1. As restrictions on the movement of labor and capital are relaxed in the world, which of the following would be expected for labor-rich countries like China?
a) Outward migration of labor.
b) Outward movement of direct capital.
c) A reduction in wages.
d) An increase in the real return to capital (real interest rate).

2. A vertically integrated firm is one that
a) Supplies inputs to other firms.
b) Buys its inputs from other firms.
c) Supplies some of its own inputs.
d) Sells its output domestically.

3. Which of the following best describes direct investment?
a) Residents of one nation purchase stocks and bonds issued in another nation.
b) Residents of one nation directly deposits fund in a bank account in another nation.
c) Residents of one nation purchase stocks and bonds in their own nation.
d) Residents of one nation own a controlling interest in a factory in another nation.

4. The movement of labor from low-wage areas to high-wage areas will
a) Lower everyone's wages.
b) Raise wages in the low-wage areas.
c) Will be favored by labor groups in the high-age areas.
d) Leave world output unchanged.

5. MNC's are firms that
a) Diversify their portfolios by buying small amounts of stocks in many firms.
b) Export to foreign-owned firms.
c) Control production in other nations.
d) Import from foreign-owned firms.

6. Portfolio risk can be improved by buying foreign assets when which of the following is true?
a) Foreign and domestic returns move opposite of one another.
b) Foreign and domestic returns move together.
c) Returns on foreign and domestic assets are very similar.
d) Foreign returns are higher than domestic returns.

7. One reason why host nations are critical of MNC activity is that MNC's
a) Export jobs.
b) Export technology.
c) Produce an outflow of capital.
d) Significantly Influence tastes and culture.

8. One reason for the existence of multinational corporations is
a) Equality of wages throughout the world.
b) Its effect on the balance of payments.
c) Economies of scale.
d) Brain drain.

9. Expansion that occurs when a firm buys or builds factories abroad to produce more of its product is
a) Portfolio investment.
b) Horizontal integration.
c) Vertical integration.
d) Transfer pricing.

10. Transfer pricing refers to the practice of MNC's when
a) Pricing labor.
b) Pricing portfolio capital.
c) Pricing productive inputs.
d) Pricing products shipped between branches of a firm.

Problems and Discussion Questions

1. a) Explain how direct investment in Mexico by MNC's located in the US can be explained by the Heckscher-Ohlin model of trade.

b) Explain how the Heckscher-Ohlin model of trade can explain the movement of labor from Mexico to the United States.

c) What effect will the movement of labor and capital have on real returns to these two factors across countries?

d) Suppose movements of labor and capital are restricted, but goods and services trade freely. What effects will these restrictions have on the real returns to labor and capital across countries?

2. a) How does the movement of labor from Mexico to the United States and the movement of capital from the US to Mexico affect world output?

b) What effect will the international movement of labor and capital between Mexico and the US have on the distribution of income within the Mexico and the United States?

3. a) Why might countries wish to curb the foreign direct investment activities of its own MNC's?

b) Why might host countries wish to curb foreign direct investment?

4. Why are MNCs often able to produce more cheaply and sell at a lower price than local firms?

5. We observe financial capital moving in two directions, i.e., funds move from the United Kingdom to the United States at the same time that funds move from the United States to the United Kingdom.
a) Can this be explained by funds seeking the higher rate of return?

b) How does the principle of risk diversification explain this two-way movement of financial capital?

6. What effect will freer trade with Mexico have on Mexican migration to the United States and on the movement of US capital to Mexico?

Part Four: The Balance of Payments, Foreign Exchange Markets, and Exchange Rates

Chapter 10
Balance of Payments

Chapter Outline

Chapter Summary and Review

Balance of Payments

The **balance of payments** is a summary of a nation's international transactions over some period of time. Examples of international transactions include the export of iPods from the US to Germany, the imports of cheese from Italy by US grocers, and the movement of funds from one nation to another. The distinction between a domestic transaction and an international transaction, however, is not always obvious. Does the sale of goods by a Sears' store in Mexico City count as US exports because Sears is headquartered in Chicago? Is the sale of a book in Cambridge, MA to a visitor from the United Kingdom an export?

For balance of payments purposes, an entity is classified as domestic or foreign according to its normal residence or location. According to this definition, the Sears store is normally located in Mexico and its sales to Mexicans are not US exports. The visitor from the United Kingdom, who normally lives in the United Kingdom, is a foreigner and the sale of the book is an export, although such sales may be difficult to capture in the balance of payments statistics.

If the United States exports goods, then buyers in other countries will have to deliver dollars to the United States. Foreigners can acquire those dollars in a number of ways. One way is to earn them by selling goods to the United States – imports of the United States. Here, the outflow and inflow of dollars due to the movement of goods are equal. Another possibility is that foreigners can sell US assets they have acquired in the past. In this case the outflow (from the US) of dollars from the sale of the asset matches the inflow of dollars due to US exports. Another possibility is to borrow US funds. In this case the outflow due to foreign borrowing matches the inflow of dollars due to the export.

The point is that every international transaction has a matching inflow and outflow. If foreigners buy goods from the United States, there must be an outflow of dollars to foreigners in order to fund the inflow of dollars to buy the goods. If US citizens import goods, then there must be an inflow of foreign currency in order for an outflow to take place to pay for the imports.

Double Entry Bookkeeping

This matching of inflows and outflows for every international transaction means that every entry recording an inflow (outflow) in the balance of payments has an accompanying entry that records an outflow (inflow). This is the nature of **double-entry bookkeeping**. Transactions that give rise to a receipt of payments from foreigners are recorded as **credits** and carry a "+" sign. Transactions that give rise to payments to foreigners are recorded as **debits** and carry a "-" sign.

Exports give rise to an inflow of funds so they will be recorded as a credit. Imports give rise to an outflow so they will be recorded as a debit. Less clear is the treatment of financial assets. When financial assets are bought or sold, there is a flow of financial capital, which is recorded as a **capital outflow** or a **capital inflow**. A capital inflow for the US occurs whenever a foreigner buys assets in the US or when a US citizen liquidates a foreign asset. A capital outflow occurs when a US citizen buys a foreign asset, or when a foreigner sells a US asset.

Consider a few examples. In each example, the recording of the transaction is viewed from the US balance of payments perspective.

Example 1: A US exporter sells $1,000 in goods to a UK firm that pays for the goods by liquidating a US Treasury Bill. The export gives rise to an inflow and is recorded as a credit, while the sale of the US Treasury bill by foreigners means an outflow of funds (in the current period) and is recorded as a debit. The transaction is shown in Table 1.

Table 1

	Credit (+)	Debit (-)
Exports	$1,000	
Capital Outflow		$1,000

Example 2: A US exporter sells $1,000 of goods to a UK firm that pays for the goods by buying dollars from its bank in London. The export, as in Example 1, is a credit. The bank in London, by selling its dollars, is liquidating its holdings of US assets (dollars), and constitutes an outflow from the US. The entry in this example is identical to that of Example 1.

Example 3: A US importer buys $5,000 of wine from a French exporter, paying for the wine by borrowing francs in Paris. The import produces an outflow of funds and is recorded as a debit. The borrowing of francs in Paris is a capital inflow, and is recorded as a credit. The lender in Paris is lending to a US citizen. The transaction is shown in Table 2.

Table 2

	Credit (+)	Debit (-)
Imports		$5,000
Capital Inflow	$5,000	

Example 4: A German bank buys a $10,000 US Treasury bill and pays by liquidating its account at a US bank. The purchase of the US Treasury bill is a capital inflow for the US and is recorded as a credit. The liquidation of the US bank account by the German bank is a capital outflow and is recorded as a debit. In this case, both sides of the transaction are recorded on the capital account, shown in Table 3.

Table 3

	Credit (+)	Debit (-)
Capital Outflow		$10,000
Capital Inflow	$10,000	

Example 5: A migrant worker sends $250 to her family in Mexico. International gifts like these are called **unilateral transfers**. This transfer give rise to an outflow and the receipt of funds in Mexico means someone in Mexico now holds dollars. The holding of dollars is a claim on the United States and so is a capital inflow. The transaction is shown in Table 4.

Table 4

	Credit (+)	Debit (-)
Unilateral Transfers		$250
Capital Inflow	$250	

The Meaning of Deficits and Surpluses in the Balance of Payments Accounts

Although the actual balance of payments is quite complex and includes millions of entries, double-entry bookkeeping means that the sum of all credits (+) must equal the sum of all debits (-). *The balance of payments always balances. In this respect, it is nonsense to talk of a balance of payments deficit or surplus. It is only meaningful to speak of deficits or surpluses for subsets of the entire balance of payments.*

The balance of debits and credits for exports and imports of goods is called the **balance of trade**, or the **merchandise trade balance**. The balance of debits and credits for exports and imports of goods and services is called the **balance of trade in goods and services**. If a balance is struck for goods and services, net investment income and unilateral transfers, then that balance is the balance on **current account**. All current account items are those that affect the source or disposition of current income.

The items left after the current account balance are **capital account** items. The capital account includes net flows of stocks, bonds, and the purchase of foreign companies. Note that because the entire balance of payments must balance, a deficit on current account means a surplus on capital account, and vice versa.

There is, however, a meaningful sense in which a nation's balance of payments can be in surplus or deficit. The items in the current account and capital account undertaken by the private sector are privately motivated, or are motivated by something other than the balance of payments itself. These items are called **autonomous transactions** because they are autonomous of, or not motivated by, the state of the balance of payments. There can be a balance of payments deficit or surplus for autonomous transactions. If autonomous transactions produce, for example, a deficit, it means that autonomous outflows exceed autonomous inflows. In light of the above discussion about double-entry bookkeeping, how can this happen? It can happen if the autonomous outflow is offset by an inflow produced by government through its **official reserve account**, the balance of which is called the **official settlements balance**. Official reserve transactions are called **accommodating transactions** because they allow (accommodate) a mismatch of credits and debits from autonomous transactions. If government refrains from reserve (accommodating) transactions, then autonomous transactions must net to zero. This will be explained in more detail when the foreign exchange market is introduced in the next chapter.

The capital account of the US balance of payments shows the yearly (or quarterly) *changes* in US assets held abroad and foreign assets held in the US. The **international investment position** shows the sum total of all those past changes. If, for example, there were a net capital inflow of $1,000 to a country from foreign nations for all twenty years of its existence, then that country would owe a total of $20,000 to foreigners. The $20,000 debt would be the international investment position of the country.

Beginning in the early to mid-1980s, the United States ran large current account deficits, which implies large capital account surpluses (official reserve movements being small). Capital account surpluses mean that the United States is borrowing from other countries. These large capital account surpluses were responsible for turning the United States from a creditor nation to a debtor nation by 1990.

Key Terms used in Chapter Summary and Review
(The list below is not necessarily the same as the list provided by the Salvatore text.)

Accommodating transactions	Credits
Autonomous transactions	Current account
Balance of payments	Debits
Balance of trade (Merchandise trade balance)	Double-entry bookkeeping
Balance of trade in goods and services	International investment position
Capital account	Official reserve account
Capital inflow	Official settlements balance
Capital outflow	Unilateral transfers

Multiple Choice Questions

1. The balance of payments is a record of
a) Exports and imports of goods.
b) Exports and imports of goods and services.
c) Exports and imports of goods and services and interest receipts.
d) All international transactions.

2. A French citizen buys a computer from an IBM branch in Belgium. This transaction
a) Is recorded as a credit in the US export account.
b) Is recorded as a debit in the Belgian export account.
c) Is recorded as a credit in the French import account.
d) Does not affect the US balance of payments.

3. According to double-entry bookkeeping, a balance of payments deficit
a) Cannot occur.
b) Occurs when debits exceed credits.
c) Occurs when credits exceed debits.
d) Will be caused by excessive imports.

4. A US importer buys goods from Mexico by borrowing pesos in Mexico City. Which of the following are the correct accounting entries?
a) Import credit; capital inflow.
b) Import credit; capital outflow.
c) Import debit; capital inflow.
d) Import debit; capital outflow.

5. A current account deficit occurs when
a) This balance of payments is negative.
b) Exports of goods are less than imports of goods.
c) There is a net capital outflow.
d) The capital account is in surplus.

6. If there is a deficit due to the autonomous transactions in the balance of payments then there must be
a) A surplus in accommodating transactions.
b) A net capital outflow.
c) A net capital inflow.
d) A trade deficit.

7. If there is a current account deficit then which of the following must also be true?
a) The capital account is in deficit.
b) The trade account is in surplus.
c) The trade account is in deficit.
d) The international investment position has decreased.

8. Assume a nation has a balance of trade deficit and its total balance of payments credits are $32 billion? The nation's balance of payments debits are:
a) Negative.
b) Equal to $32 billion.
c) Less than $32 billion.
d) More than $32 billion.

9. What does the US trade deficit with China necessarily mean?
a) China is lending to the US.
b) The US is a net investor in China.
c) US consumers buy more Chinese products than US products.
d) The production of Chinese producers exceeds that of US producers.

10. Transactions that give rise to payments to foreigners are
a) Credits.
b) Exports.
c) US purchases of foreign stocks.
d) Foreign purchases of US stocks.

Problems and Discussion Questions

1. Record the following US balance of payments transactions, using entries like those shown in Tables 1-4 of the Chapter Summary and Review.
a) The US exports $500 of computers to France, with payment to take place in three months.

b) The US imports $400 of goods from the U.K., making immediate payment by buying pounds from a U.K. bank.

c) You travel to the U.K. for holiday and spend $300.

d) The US gives aid of $200 to a developing country.

e) A US citizen buys $100 of stock (a long-term asset) in Belgium. Belgian Euros are purchased from a US bank.

f) A U.K. citizen buys a $50 short-term US Treasury bill. The U.K. citizen buys the dollars from a US bank.

2. a) Using the transactions you recorded in Question 1, fill in the US Balance of Payments table below. Note that a number of the transactions you recorded in Question 1 involved short-term capital, so it's useful to net all the short-term capital debits and credits into one number.

US Balance of Payments

Account	Credit (+)	Debit (-)
Merchandise Exports		
Merchandise Imports		
Tourist Services		
Unilateral Transfers		
Long-Term Capital		
Short-Term Capital		
Balance		

Based on the table in part a), calculate the following US balances.

b) The Balance of trade.

c) The Balance of trade in goods and services.

d) The Balance on current account.

e) The Balance on capital account.

f) Is the entire US balance of payments in the above table in deficit or surplus?

3. a) In what sense is it meaningless to speak of a balance of payments surplus or deficit?

b) In what sense is it meaningful to speak of a balance of payments surplus or deficit?

4. Based on the balances found in Question 2, calculate the change in the international investment position of the US.

5. a) How has the US balance of payments and its international investment position changed, beginning in the mid-1980s?

b) What are the benefits associated with the change in the US international investment position you described in part a)?

c) What might be the costs of the change in the US international investment position you described in part a)?

Chapter 11
The Foreign Exchange Market and Exchange Rates

Chapter Outline

Chapter Summary and Review

The Foreign Exchange Market and Equilibrium Exchange Rates

One of the parties involved in an international transaction must deal in foreign currency. If a US exporter sells goods, where the contract is stated in foreign currency, then the US exporter will receive foreign currency and will eventually exchange the foreign currency for dollars. If the US exporter's contract is stated in dollars, then the foreign buyer must buy dollars with foreign currency. Note that no matter what the currency of denomination, US exports produce a sale of foreign currency and a purchase of dollars. Similarly, US imports will produce a sale of dollars and a purchase of foreign currency.

The exchange of dollars and foreign currencies takes place on the **foreign exchange market**. The foreign exchange market consists of all the banks and foreign exchange dealers around the world where currencies can be traded. Dollars can be exchanged for **Euros** in Tokyo, London, and Bonn, as well as in New York and Paris. The **exchange rate** can be expressed as the price in dollars of foreign currency (number of dollars per one unit of foreign currency) or its inverse, the price in foreign currency of the dollar (number of units of foreign currency for one dollar). Because one is the inverse of the other, it is immaterial which is used, but it is standard to express the exchange rate as the dollar cost of foreign currency.

Thus the exchange rate, R, for the British pound will be defined as

$$R = \$/\pounds.$$

If $R = 1.5$, then it costs $1.50 to buy one British pound.

The number of pounds sold on the foreign exchange market in any time period is determined by the willingness of owners of pounds, including U.K. residents as well as anyone else who owns pounds, to sell (supply) their pounds for dollars at a particular exchange rate. As the exchange rate increases (more dollars per pound) the quantity supplied will increase because to owners of pounds, it appears as if goods and assets have become cheaper. A candy bar that costs $1 in the United States will cost pound holders £1 when $R=1$, but will cost pound holders only one-half of a pound when $R=2$. Therefore, as R increases those individuals who own pounds will purchase more goods and assets in the United States. An increased R increases the quantity supplied of pounds to buy things in the US, producing the upward sloping supply, $S_\pounds$, in Figure 11.1.

The demand curve for pounds, $D_\pounds$ in Fig. 11.1, is downward sloping because as the dollar cost of pounds decreases, it appears to those with dollars that goods and assets in the United Kingdom are cheaper, motivating increased purchases of U.K. goods and assets, and an increased quantity demanded for pounds.

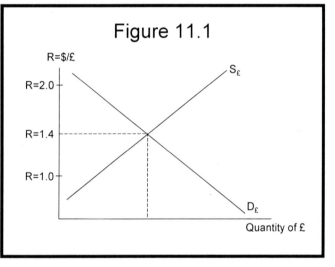

In a **flexible exchange–rate system (floating-rate system)**, the price of foreign currency is determined solely by market conditions, and so will move to equate the quantity supplied and quantity demanded, which occurs at $R=1.4$ in Fig. 11.1. The pound will increase (**appreciate),** or decrease (**depreciate)** as the demand and supply schedules shift. A shift to the right of the demand for pounds (increased demand for pounds) or a shift to the left in the supply of pounds (a decrease in the supply of pounds) will cause the pound to appreciate – increase in value to a higher dollar cost per pound. A shift to the left of the demand for pounds or a shift to the right of the supply curve will cause the pound to depreciate – decrease in value to a lower dollar cost. Note that an appreciation of the pound is equivalent to a depreciation of the dollar.

The popular press often draws attention to the change in the value of a currency relative to one of its trading partners, e.g., a depreciation of the dollar with respect to the Japanese yen or the euro. Although such bilateral exchange rates are important, exchange rates should also be considered relative to all trading partners. The general value of a currency is measured by **effective exchange rates**, which is a weighted average of the value with respect to all other currencies, where the weights are usually determined by the relative importance of trade with each of the other nations.

Although many currencies can be purchased in many different financial centers, the cost of any one currency is the same in all locales due to **arbitrage**. Arbitrage is the simultaneous purchase and sale of any asset. If a pound is cheap in Paris, but expensive in London, then arbitragers will buy pounds in Paris and simultaneously sell them in London, profiting from the difference. The act of buying in the cheap market will cause the cheap rate to rise, and the act of selling in the expensive market will cause the expensive rate to fall, until the rates are identical except for small transaction costs, which are usually very small. Arbitrage can also occur across three or more financial centers. If dollars bought with francs in Paris can be converted to marks in New York cheaper than directly using dollars to buy marks in Frankfurt, then arbitragers can profit from the difference, and will cause rates to be consistent everywhere in the world.

The supply and demand curves for foreign currency represent the autonomous balance of payments transactions described in Chapter 10. The autonomous transactions represent the intentions of the private sector to buy and sell goods and assets in the foreign market, which in this case is the United Kingdom. If, in a floating-rate system, the demand for pounds increases from $D_£$ to $D_£'$, as shown in Figure 11.2, the pound will appreciate to R=2.

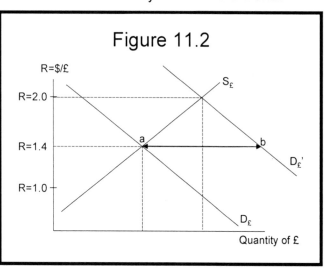

Figure 11.2

If, however, a nation wishes to pursue a **fixed exchange–rate system** and keep the exchange rate fixed at R=1.4, then the monetary authorities must intervene in the foreign exchange market. At R=1.4, there is an excess demand for pounds equal to the distance **ab**. In order to keep the exchange rate from moving this excess demand for pounds must be supplied by the monetary authorities. Either the United States authorities must supply pounds (and buy dollars) from its inventory of pounds or the authorities of the United Kingdom must supply pounds and add to its inventories of dollars. These inventories of foreign exchange maintained by the monetary authority in each nation are called foreign exchange **reserves**.

At R=1.4, the excess autonomous demand for pounds is equivalent to a deficit in the official settlements balance for the United States because there is a desired outflow of dollars that exceeds the desired inflow (an excess demand for pounds is an excess supply of dollars).

The United States could opt for a combination of a change in the exchange rate and a use of reserves, limiting the exchange rate to something in between R=1.4 and R=2.0. An exchange rate system in which some combination of exchange rate systems and intervention is used is called a **managed floating exchange–rate system**.

In a floating–rate system, the exchange rate continually adjusts to produce an equality of outflows of a currency (quantity supplied) and inflows of a currency (quantity demanded), so the balance of payments for all autonomous transactions net to zero.

Foreign Exchange Risk and Speculation

The exchange rate in Fig. 11.2 is the cost of currency for immediate (on-the-spot) delivery and is referred to as the **spot rate**. There are a number of other types of foreign exchange transactions and instruments that are used by traders and investors to accomplish their objectives. One of these is the **forward market** in foreign exchange. A forward transaction in the foreign exchange market is an agreement to buy or sell foreign exchange at a *current* price for future delivery. For example, the current spot rate for pounds may be R=1.4, while the current **forward rate**, FR, might be FR=1.39. This says that the pound may be bought or sold at today's forward rate of $1.39/£, with settlement to occur in the future. Standard maturities of forward contracts are for one month, three months and six months. If you agree to buy pounds in the one–month forward market and the current forward rate is FR=$1.39/£, then in one month you will be obligated to buy pounds and deliver $1.39 per pound bought. Notice that the forward rate locks in a price that does not change no matter what happens to the spot rate over the next month.

If the forward rate is less than the current spot rate, then forward currency is said to be selling at a **forward discount**. If the forward rate exceeds the current spot rate, then forward currency is selling at a **forward premium**. Forward discounts and premiums are often expressed as a percentage of the spot rate, with an adjustment for the time period to express the result on an annual basis.

A **currency swap** is a combination of a spot transaction and a forward transaction. In a currency swap, one party agrees to sell a currency at the current spot rate and to buy it back in the future at a price agreed upon today. (The other party to the transaction agrees to do the opposite.) Currency swaps can be ongoing rather than one-time transactions, meaning that the parties to the transaction agree to continually swap currencies every month. Ongoing currency swaps are equivalent to a series of spot and forward transactions. Currency swaps, especially ongoing currency swaps, are useful because the series of transactions are agreed to in one contract, which produces smaller transaction costs than a series of separate spot and forward transactions.

Foreign currency futures are equivalent to forward currency transactions. The principal difference is that futures are standardized with respect to the date at which the contract matures (rather than the length of maturity) and the size of the transaction. Futures transactions can also be satisfied -"undone"- at any point before maturity while forward positions must be maintained until maturity.

Foreign exchange options are similar to forward and futures transactions in that they allow future transactions at prices negotiated today, but they do differ in one crucial respect. Options confer the *right* to sell (a put option) or buy (a call option) foreign exchange in the future, but not the obligation to buy or sell. That is, futures and forward contracts must be honored, but options can be allowed to lapse without completing the transaction. (Sellers of options must honor if the buyer chooses.) The right to buy or sell, however, costs the buyer of an option a price (generally ranging from 1 to 5% of the value of the contract), whereby a futures contract has no inherent price,

Forward, futures, swap, and options transactions in the foreign exchange market are examples of derivative instruments, and, like any derivative market, allow two basic types of strategies by participants in the market. First, they allow traders and investors to **hedge** their foreign exchange positions. Hedging is the use of instruments to reduce the risk of a transaction. For example, a US exporter may sell to a French firm, where the terms of the contract give the French firm 30 days to deliver the agreed upon number of Euros. (It is assumed that the contract is denominated in Euros.) The US exporter is exposed to **foreign exchange risk** because the euro may depreciate by the time Euros are delivered. If the euro converts into fewer dollars than anticipated, then the exporter may realize a loss on the sale of goods to the French firm. In this case, the US exporter is "open" to exchange fluctuations. The exporter can "close," or hedge, the exposure in a number of ways by using foreign exchange derivatives.

One strategy is to *sell* the anticipated euro proceeds on the forward or futures market. Recall that a forward contract allows the sale (or purchase) of currency at a rate agreed upon today. Thus the exporter can lock in a price in the forward market. When the Euros are received, they can be converted to dollars at the previously contracted forward rate. If the current forward rate is acceptable to the firm, then the goods can be exported with no fear of a change in the exchange rate. The forward contract does, though, eliminate the gains from any favorable change in the spot exchange rate, as well as the losses from unfavorable changes in the spot exchange rate.

The US exporter could also buy the option to sell foreign exchange (buy a put) at a particular price. If the exchange rate turns against the importer, then the option could be exercised. If the change in the spot exchange rate is favorable, then the option could be allowed to lapse and the Francs sold at the favorable spot rate. Remember, though, there is a cost to the option that must be paid, much like an insurance premium that must be paid whether an insurance claim is made or not.

Hedging eliminates exchange risk through the use of forward, futures and options contracts. These derivatives are also excellent vehicles for assuming risk, which is **speculation**. If you expect the pound to appreciate, you can speculate in the pound by buying it now and waiting for it to appreciate. Buying pounds outright, however, requires a current use of funds. You can speculate on an appreciation of the pound much more cheaply by buying pounds in the forward or futures market, or by buying a call option on pounds. If the pound appreciates, then you can buy at the contracted price stipulated in the forward, futures or options contract, and sell at the higher spot rate.

Speculators can serve a very useful function in foreign exchange markets. If speculators are correct, on average, about the future movements of a currency, then they will buy when the currency is low and sell when it is high. Buying at a low price will increase the price and selling when it is high lowers the price. Thus, if speculation is on average correct, it will reduce the peaks and valleys of exchange rate movements. Such speculation is **stabilizing speculation**. If, on the other hand, speculators sell when the currency is low, making its value even lower, and buy when it is high, making its value even higher, then speculation is **destabilizing speculation**.

Interest Arbitrage

When speculation occurs in the spot market, buying a currency when the value of the currency is expected to increase in value, the foreign exchange purchased is not held in bank notes. Rather, it is held in the form of interest-bearing deposit accounts. Thus speculators must consider not only the changes in the value of a currency, but also the interest rate in foreign markets relative to the interest rate that could be earned in the home market. Taking advantage of differences in interest rates and expected changes in currency values is called **uncovered interest arbitrage**, uncovered referring to the fact that such transactions are *exposed* to exchange risk.

Letting i* be the foreign interest rate, the expected return on a foreign interest bearing asset is

$$i^* + [E(SR)-SR]/SR$$

SR is the current spot rate and E(SR) is the expected spot rate when the foreign asset matures. [E(SR)-SR]/SR is the expected gain (or loss) on the foreign exchange conversion from buying and selling a foreign asset, expressed as a fraction of the spot rate. If you buy a foreign asset when the spot rate is SR=1.4, and expect to sell your foreign exchange at maturity at a value of 1.5, then E(SR)=1.5, and the gain from currency conversion is [1.5-1.4]/1.4 = .071, or 7.1% is the expected gain from currency conversion. If the foreign interest rate is 5%, then the expected gain on a foreign deposit is 12.1%. If this exceeds the domestic interest rate, i, then funds will flow abroad. If the domestic interest rate exceeds 12.1%, then funds will flow to the domestic market. **Uncovered interest parity** occurs when the two are equal, i.e.,

$$i = i^* + [E(SR)-SR]]/SR.$$

Suppose $i < i^* + [E(SR)-SR]/SR$. Funds will flow abroad causing an increased demand for foreign currency, which will cause the spot rate, SR, to increase. As R increases, $[E(SR)-SR]/SR$ will decrease, causing the right-hand side of the equality to decrease. In addition the increased supply of funds abroad will cause i^* to fall which also cause the right-hand of the inequality to decrease. The outflow of funds (reduced supply) from domestic markets will cause i to increase. The movements of i, i^*, and SR will continue until uncovered interest parity holds. Uncovered interest parity can only be expected to be approximately true because the expected spot rate is not known with certainty, so investors may require an exchange-risk premium to enter into the risky transaction. (In general, the riskier is any transaction the greater is the return required by an investor to compensate for that risk.)

Investors in foreign assets could choose to eliminate foreign exchange risk. Instead of buying a foreign asset and remaining open to exchange rate changes, the expected proceeds can be sold in the forward market at a known forward rate. In this case the proceeds will be sold at the forward rate, indicated by FR. Now the return on a foreign investment is

$$i^* + [FR-SR]/SR.$$

Because FR is known at the time of the transaction, the return, including the return from selling the proceeds at the forward rate and buying at the spot rate is known with certainty. Now if $i < i^* + [FR-SR]/SR$, then funds will flow abroad, causing an increased demand in the spot market, causing SR to increase as before. In addition, there will be increased sales in the forward market, causing FR to decrease. Both the change in FR and SR will cause $[FR-SR]/SR$ to decrease. This, along with the effect of the movement of funds on the interest rates described above will continue until

$$i = i^* + [FR-SR]/SR.$$

This equality is called **covered interest arbitrage parity (CIAP)**, or **covered interest rate parity**. Because there is no uncertainty associated with the foreign investment, covered interest rate parity can be expected to hold precisely, except for small transaction costs. Empirical evidence does support the existence of covered interest arbitrage parity.

Key Terms used in Chapter Summary and Review

(The list below is not necessarily the same as the list provided by the Salvatore text.)

Arbitrage

Appreciate

Covered interest arbitrage parity

Covered interest rate parity

Currency swap

Depreciate

Destabilizing speculation

Effective exchange rates

Euros

Exchange rate

Fixed exchange–rate system

Flexible exchange–rate system

Floating-rate system

Foreign currency futures

Forward discount

Forward market

Forward rate

Foreign exchange market

Foreign exchange options

Foreign exchange risk

Forward premium

Hedge

Managed floating exchange–rate system

Reserves

Speculation

Spot rate

Stabilizing speculation

Uncovered interest arbitrage

Uncovered interest parity

Multiple Choice Questions

1. An increase in the demand for the dollar by European residents in a fixed exchange-rate system will lead to
a) A depreciation of the dollar.
b) A depreciation of the euro.
c) Sales of the dollar by the government in the US or in Europe.
d) Purchases of the dollar by the government in the US or in Europe.

2. An increase in the demand for the dollar by European residents in a floating exchange-rate system will lead to
a) A depreciation of the dollar.
b) A depreciation of the euro.
c) Sales of the dollar by the government in US or Europe.
d) Purchases of the dollar by the government in US or Europe.

3. A currency swap is the
a) Exchange of one currency for another in the spot market.
b) The exchange of currency in the spot market and the forward market.
c) The purchase of foreign exchange options.
d) The purchase of foreign exchange futures.

4. If you expect a royalty from your publisher in London, payable in pounds, then you can hedge your foreign exchange risk by
a) Buying a foreign exchange option to buy pounds.
b) Selling dollars for pounds on the forward exchange market.
c) Selling pounds for dollars on the forward exchange market.
d) Waiting to see what happens to the value of the pound on the spot market.

5. If the interest rate on deposits in Europe yield 3% and the euro is expected to appreciate 1%, then if there is uncovered arbitrage the US interest rate must be
a) 1%.
b) 2%.
c) 3%.
d) 4%.

6. The interest rate on deposits in Europe is 5%, while in the US it is 2%. Which of the following must be true?
a) The demand for Euros will increase.
b) The forward discount on Euros is 3%.
c) The forward premium on Euros is 3%.
d) The euro is expected to appreciate.

7. As a result of arbitrage
a) Forward and spot rates will be identical.
b) Forward and expected spot rates will be identical.
c) The forward rate will be above the spot rate.
d) The dollar will cost the same number of Euros in Frankfort and Ottawa.

8. As a result of the action of successful speculators in the foreign exchange market
a) Exchange rates will be more stable.
b) Foreign exchange markets will not reach equilibrium.
c) Exchange rate risk will be greater for international transactions.
d) Hedging will no longer be appropriate for covering foreign exchange risk.

9. If the euro appreciates relative to the dollar, then
a) US investors with holdings of European financial assets will lose.
b) European investors with holdings of US financial assets will gain.
c) Those with Euros will want to sell more Euros to buy dollars.
d) Prices in Europe will appear to be lower to US residents.

10. Which of the following must be true given the following: Mexican interest rate = 4%, US interest rate = 4%, one dollar buys 10 pesos?
a) The peso is expected to depreciate.
b) The peso is selling at a forward discount.
c) One dollar is worth 10 pesos on the forward market.
d) Funds will move from Mexico to the Unites States.

Problems and Discussion Questions

1. Assume that the foreign exchange market is initially in equilibrium. What effect will each of the following changes have on the dollar value of the yen ($/¥) if exchange rates are allowed to float freely? Use foreign exchange supply and demand curves for yen to explain each answer separately.
a) An increase in interest rates in Japan

b) Lowered incomes in the US (recession).

c) A reduction in import barriers in Japan

d) An increase in inflation in the U. S.

2. a) Use uncovered interest parity combined with covered interest parity to show what the relationship is between the expected future spot rate and the current forward rate.

b) In a) you found the implied relationship between the expected future spot rate and the current forward rate. What is the behavior on the part of investors that will cause this relationship to hold?

c) Do you think the relationship that you found in part a) is precise? Why?

3. Suppose IBM sells computers in Japan and receives revenues in yen. IBM's expenses however are in dollars.
a) Does IBM risk an appreciation or depreciation of the yen?

b) What can IBM do in the forward market to eliminate the risk you described in part a)?

c) What can IBM do in the swap market to eliminate the risk of part a)?

4. a) The dollar price of British pounds in Tokyo and Bonn are shown in the table below.

<u>Tokyo</u>   <u>Bonn</u>
R = $/£ = 1.45   R = $/£ = 1.40

Explain why the above is a disequilibrium situation, and what will happen to force the two prices towards equality.

b) Exchange rates in three financial centers are shown in the table below.

<u>New York</u>   <u>London</u>   <u>Paris</u>
R = $/£ = 1.45   R = $/Euro = .20   R = Euro/£ = 7

If you have dollars and are interested in buying pounds, where would you obtain them?

c) Explain why the situation presented in the table in part b) is a disequilibrium situation, and what will happen.

5. Describe three ways to bet on your forecast of an increase in the dollar value of the yen.

6. Describe the forward transaction necessary to hedge the transactions described below.
a) A U.K. firm imports wine from Germany, agreeing to deliver Euros in thirty days.

b) A US bank lends dollars to a French bank and agrees to accept Euros in thirty days.

c) A Canadian investor buys a one-year US government security.

d) A US firm borrows Japanese yen and agrees to repay the yen in ninety days.

e) A US importer expects to receive Japanese yen in thirty days and borrows an equivalent amount of yen in Tokyo today, and converts the yen to dollars today.

7. Suppose $i > i^* + [FR-SR]/SR$. How will interest arbitragers respond and what effect will this have on the inequality?

Chapter 12
Exchange Rate Determination

Chapter Outline

Chapter Summary and Review

Equilibrium Exchange Rates

In Chapter 11, a very general explanation of the equilibrium exchange rate was developed. That framework consisted of a private demand and private supply curve of foreign exchange, whose intersection determine the equilibrium exchange rate in a floating exchange-rate system. That equilibrium will be disturbed, producing a new equilibrium exchange rate if anything causes the supply curve to shift, or the demand curve to shift.

The demand for foreign exchange is the desire of those who hold dollars to sell their dollars in return for foreign exchange. If that desire increases, the demand curve for foreign exchange will shift to the right. A rightward shift of the demand curve for foreign exchange would create an excess demand for foreign exchange at the old exchange rate, which would lead to an appreciation of foreign exchange (the dollars needed to buy one unit of foreign exchange would increase.) There are many factors that could cause the demand for foreign exchange to shift to the right, the most common of which are:

• Increases in domestic income, which increases imports, and so the demand for foreign exchange
• Decreases in domestic interest rates, which increases the demand for foreign assets, and so the demand for foreign exchange.

- Increases in domestic inflation, which increases the demand for now relatively cheaper imports, and so the demand for foreign exchange.
- The expectation that foreign exchange will appreciate, which increases the demand for foreign currency, which investors expect to increase in value (worth more dollars.)

All of the above changes can also be reversed, which decreases the demand for foreign exchange and results in a depreciation of the foreign currency.

The supply of foreign currency is the desire of those who hold foreign currency to exchange it for dollars. If the desire increases, then the supply curve will shift to the right. A rightward shift of the supply curve would create excess supply of foreign exchange, resulting in a depreciation of foreign currency. The most common factors that would increase the amount of foreign exchange sold for dollars are:

- An increase in foreign income, which increases imports by foreign residents, requiring a sale of foreign currency to buy the imports.
- An increase in foreign inflation, which increases imports by foreign residents, requiring a sale of foreign currency to buy the imports.
- A decrease in foreign interest rates, which produces a flow of capital from foreign residents to the US, requiring a sale of foreign currency.
- An expected appreciation of the dollar, producing a speculative supply of foreign currency.

Of course many or all of the above regularly occur simultaneously and the effect on the exchange rate is the net effect of all of the supply and demand shifts.

Although the above framework is general enough to describe how exchange rates are determined, some of the forces are at work in the short run and some in the long run, motivating a number of different approaches to the determination of exchange rates. The different approaches to exchange rate determination are described below.

Elasticity Approach
The **elasticity approach** is based on the flow of goods –trade- between nations. In this approach, the demand and supply of foreign exchange are determined by the demand for imports and the supply of exports. If something increases the demand for imports (such as an increase in domestic income), then there will be an excess demand for foreign exchange at the old exchange rate, so foreign currency will appreciate. The appreciation will cause the quantity demanded to decrease and the quantity supplied to increase until there is equilibrium at a higher price for foreign currency. How much foreign currency appreciates depends upon how responsive (elastic) the demand and supply of foreign currency, which depends upon how responsive imports and exports are to changes in the exchange rate.

Purchasing-Power Parity Approach

Purchasing-power parity is also based on the flow of goods. The **Purchasing-Power Parity (PPP) Theory** takes two forms: **absolute PPP** and **relative PPP**. Both forms originate from the idea that a dollar will be able to buy the same amount of goods anywhere in the world. If it could not, then substitution will cause the exchange rates and/or prices to change to equalize the purchasing power. Suppose, for example, that a dollar purchased more goods in Europe than in the United States. The resulting high demand for the Euro and European goods would cause the price of the Euro to increase and the price of European goods to increase (and the price of US goods to decrease), until the purchasing power of the dollar was the same in both Europe and the US

Absolute PPP starts with the **law of one price**. If P_g^* is the price of gold (or any commodity) in Europe in Euros, and R is the dollar cost of the Euro (\$/Euro), then the price of gold in Europe, when expressed in dollars is

$$P_g = P_g^*(R).$$

The dollar cost of gold in the US, P_g, must equal $P_g^*(R)$ in equilibrium. If $P_g > P_g^*(R)$, then gold would be purchased in Europe and sold in the US, causing P_g to fall and both P_g^* and R to increase until there was equality. Thus, the law of one price states that

$$P_g = P_g^*(R) \text{ or}$$

$$R = P_g/P_g^*.$$

Thus, the exchange rate, the dollar cost of the Euro, will equal the ratio of dollar prices to prices in Europe.

When this is extended to all goods, whose prices are measured by price indices, then we have absolute PPP, i.e.,

$$R = P/P^*$$

where P is the price index in the United States and P^* is the price index in Europe.

There are two problems with PPP. First, PPP considers only the market for goods. The exchange rate is influenced not only by the supply and demand for goods, but also by movements of capital. The exchange rate will change in response to increased or reduced demand for foreign assets, and not necessarily reflect just relative price levels. The second problem is transportation costs. Some goods are so expensive to transport, e.g., land and haircuts, that they are not traded. Others are traded, but prices will differ by the cost of transportation.

Relative PPP recognizes that may R differ from P/P* due to the above considerations. But if the difference between R and P/P* is relatively constant, then *changes* in R should reflect *changes* in P and P*. Stated algebraically,

$$\%\Delta R = \%\Delta P - \%\Delta P^*.$$

This says that if the US has a higher rate of inflation than Europe ($\%\Delta P > \%\Delta P^*$), that the Euro will appreciate ($\%\Delta R > 0$). The cause of this is the substitution out of US goods into European goods. As the demand for the Euro increases, in order to buy more European goods, the Euro will appreciate.

Empirically, PPP is a reasonable description of price levels and exchange rates but only for very long periods of time, perhaps because goods markets are not highly integrated, as is assumed by PPP. It takes considerable time for goods to be substituted internationally. PPP also works best to describe inflationary periods, and not for periods in which the price of non-traded goods change relative to the price of trade goods. (Recall that it is the existence of non-traded goods that will cause deviations from PPP)

The Monetary Approach

In the trade and purchasing-power parity approaches, the exchange rate is determined by the international flow of funds to purchases goods. In the **monetary approach**, equilibrium occurs when money supply and demand are in equilibrium. If a nation has an international deficit, due to net movements of capital and goods, then there must be an excess supply of money domestically. The only way for domestic money to, net, flow out of a country is if the amount demanded domestically is less than the amount available (supplied) domestically. The opposite is true for a surplus.

Now assume that money supply equals money demand. Net, there is neither a flow out, or into the nation, so the exchange rate is in equilibrium. If, now, the money supply increases, then there will be an excess supply of money, so there must be a net outflow of money. This net outflow means an excess supply of domestic currency on the foreign exchange rate so the domestic currency will depreciate. From PPP (R = P/P*) a depreciation of the domestic currency (R increases), means spending substitution from foreign to domestic goods. Given P^*, R and P will increase by the same percentage. Thus monetary expansion in one nation will depreciate its currency and inflate its prices. In the monetary approach the principal cause of exchange rate changes are different money supply growth rates.

The Asset Approach

The **asset market,** or **portfolio balance approach,** to exchange rates views money as just one asset of many, and views the exchange rate as that which equates the supply and demand for all assets, including money and bonds. In the asset market approach, each wealth owner distributes wealth in some way between domestic money, domestic bonds and foreign bonds. Money will be held in order to conduct ongoing transactions, but there is a cost to do so in the form of foregone interest that could be earned on bonds. Thus, wealth will be balanced between money for transactions and bonds for the interest payments. Some of those bonds may be foreign bonds due to a higher return and due to possible diversification benefits. The split between money, domestic bonds and foreign bonds depends upon wealth, relative interest rates, expected appreciation (or depreciation) of the foreign currency, and risk. Because there is substitution between money, domestic bonds, and foreign bonds, a disturbance in any one of the markets can affect the exchange rate.

Exchange Rate Dynamics

In the early 1970s, the major industrial nations (e.g., Canada, Europe, Japan, and the US) moved from a relatively fixed exchange–rate system to a floating–rate system. One important characteristic of that system is very volatile exchange rates in which the exchange moves more than is necessary to reach its long-run average value, as shown in Figure 12.1. This is called "**exchange rate overshooting**", which can be explained by the asset approach.

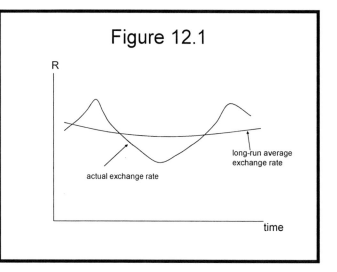

Figure 12.1

Part of the argument uses the uncovered interest parity argument from Chapter 11, which is

$$i = i^* + [E(SR)-SR]/SR.$$

The US interest rate is i, and the foreign interest rate is i^*. The term $[E(SR)-SR]/SR$ is the expected appreciation of the foreign currency. To make this visually and conceptually simpler, let this term equal EA for "expected appreciation", so

$$i = i^* + EA$$

If EA is negative then there is an expected depreciation.

Initially assume that EA = 0 so that $i=i^*$. Now assume the US money supply is increased by some percentage at time t_0 in Figure 12.2. This will cause a depreciation of the dollar (R increases) and an increase in the US price level, as explained in the

Monetary Approach above. The price level, however, moves slowly. With an increase in the money supply (not yet absorbed by an increase in prices), there is an excess supply of money which reduces the US interest rate, i.

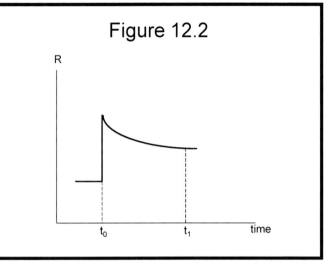

If i has fallen so that it is now below i^*, then EA must be negative – R is expected to fall. Now, combine this with the fact that the eventual increase in P will cause R to increase. This seems like a contradiction, but it can happen if the exchange rate, R, shoots up at time period t_0 as a result of the interest rate decrease in the US, and then settles down to a rate that is still above the initial rate, as shown in Fig. 12.2. Exchange rate overshooting can occur if interest rates adjust quickly and prices move slowly, as we do, in fact, observe.

Predicting Exchange Rates

Interestingly, the monetary and asset approaches to exchange rates do not perform very well in predicting exchange rates, except over very long time periods. In fact, these models are outperformed in the short run by simply assuming that exchange rates move randomly. (If exchange rates move randomly, then exchange rates will not, on average, change from the previous period.) This inability to predict exchange rates may be due to the failure of PPP to hold in the short run and from the likelihood of short-run movements of exchange rates to be dominated by day-to-day "news," which by its very nature is random. There may also be bandwagon effects, in which foreign exchange speculators fulfill their own expectations, causing exchange rates to move simply because they believe that others expect the exchange rate to move. Such behavior will produce movements of exchange rates quite independent of the underlying fundamental factors identified by the monetary and portfolio approaches.

Key Terms used in Chapter Summary and Review
(The list below is not necessarily the same as the list provided by the Salvatore text.)

Absolute PPP
Asset market approach
Elasticity approach
Exchange rate overshooting
Law of one price
Purchasing-power parity (PPP) theory

Relative PPP
Monetary approach
Portfolio balance approach
Real exchange rate
Nominal exchange rate

Multiple Choice Questions

1. If the demand and supply of foreign exchange are very elastic with respect to the exchange rate, then a shift of supply or demand in a floating-rate system will produce
a) Relatively small changes in the amount of currency traded.
b) Persistent surpluses or deficits.
c) Relatively small changes in the exchange rate.
d) Larger initial deficits and surpluses.

2. An appreciation of the foreign exchange rate will
a) Decrease the demand for foreign exchange.
b) Increased the demand for foreign exchange.
c) Increase the quantity supplied of foreign exchange.
d) Increase the quantity demanded of foreign exchange.

3. According to the elasticity approach, equilibrium exchange rates are determined by
a) The demand and supply of currencies due to trade.
b) The demand and supply of money
c) The demand and supply of bonds.
d) Relative interest rates.

4. If a Coke costs $1 in the US and .75 Euros in France, then
a) The law of one price does not apply.
b) If the law of one price applies, the cost of a Euro must be 1^{1/3}$.
c) If the law of one price applies, the cost of a Euro must be $0.75.
d) If the law of one price applies, the cost of a Euro must be $1.

5. According to the monetary approach, if two nations each increase their money supply by 10% which of the following will be most likely.
a) Both currencies will depreciate relative to each other.
b) The exchange rate between the two nations will not change
c) Both currencies will appreciate relative to each other.
d) Both currencies will undershoot.

6. Which of the following groups will gain as a result of an appreciation of the US dollar relative to the Euro?
a) German tourists who visit the US.
b) German importers.
c) US exporters.
d) US tourists who visit Italy.

7. The quantity demanded of a nation's currency increases as the currency depreciates because
a) The supply of the currency decreases.
b) The nation's goods become cheaper to foreigners.
c) Goods of the nation's trading partners become cheaper.
d) Purchasing-power parity does not hold.

8. If the dollar is expected to appreciate relative to the yen then, according to uncovered interest rate arbitrage, interest rates in the US are
a) Lower than Japanese interest rates.
b) Equal to Japanese interest rates.
c) Expected to decline.
d) Expected to increase.

9. If there is an increase in the Japanese money supply and interest rates respond before prices then,
a) The yen will depreciate quickly to its new level.
b) The yen will appreciate quickly and then gradually depreciate to a new level.
c) The yen will depreciate quickly and then gradually appreciate to a new level.
d) The yen will depreciate quickly and then gradually appreciate to its old level.

10. If there is relative purchasing power parity then
a) The Euro will buy more in Europe than elsewhere.
b) The Euro will buy the same thing everywhere in the world.
c) The Euro's purchasing power will change by the same amount everywhere in the world.
d) The Euro's purchasing power will change by a greater amount in Europe than anywhere else in the world.

Problems and Discussion Questions

1. Using supply and demand curves for foreign currency, determine the effect of the following on the dollar cost of the Euro.
a) An increase in the European interest rates.

b) Growth of incomes in Europe.

c) The dollar is expected to appreciate.

2. Using supply and demand curves for the dollar, determine the effect of the changes in Question 1 on the Euro cost of the dollar.

3. The relative average price of goods in two countries, when expressed in a common currency, e.g., dollars, is called the **real exchange rate**. For example, the real exchange rate for the yen is $(P^{¥})(R)/P^{\$}$, where $P^{¥}$ is the price level in yen, R is the dollar cost of the yen ($/¥), and $P^{\$}$ is the price level in dollars. R is the **nominal exchange rate** and is simply the spot rate.
a) If absolute PPP holds, then what is the value of the real exchange rate?

b) If absolute PPP holds, then how many candy bars will $10 buy in the United States relative to Japan?

4. a) Can the law of one price hold for all traded goods and absolute PPP not hold?

b) If absolute PPP does not hold, but relative PPP does, then what should happen to the real exchange rate over time?

c) If all goods are traded would you expect absolute PPP to hold?

5. a) Explain how the monetary approach to exchange rate determination includes the elasticity approach.

b) Explain how the asset approach to exchange rate determination includes the monetary approach.

6. a) Draw the time path of the exchange rate if an increase in the money supply is accompanied by a simultaneous and proportionately equal increase in the price level.

b) Draw the time path of the exchange rate if an increase in the money supply produces a delayed increase in the price level.

Part Five: Open-Economy Macroeconomics

Chapter 13
Automatic Adjustments with Flexible and Fixed Exchange Rates

Chapter Outline

Chapter Summary and Review

Price Adjustments in an Open Economy

As developed in Chapter 11, the foreign exchange market indicates the state of the balance of payments. If there is a surplus or deficit in the balance of payments, then there is disequilibrium in the foreign exchange market, which will result in a change in the exchange rate if exchange rates are free to vary. As the exchange rate changes, the supply and demand for foreign exchange will change. The degree to which the exchange rate must change depends upon the response of the quantity supplied and demanded for foreign exchange, or the elasticities of the supply and demand for foreign exchange with respect to the exchange rate. In this approach, the primary focus is on how exchange rate changes affect the quantity supplied and demanded of foreign exchange through the effect of exchange rate changes on trade flows. This approach to adjustment is an early approach to balance of payments adjustment known as the trade or elasticity approach, which was briefly described in Chapter 11.

In the elasticity approach, the elasticities of the supply and demand for foreign exchange rest on the underlying elasticities in the market for exports and imports. The US demand for foreign exchange, say British pounds, depends upon the US market for imports from the Britain. The US market for imports from Britain is shown in Figure 13.1, where the vertical axis measures prices in pounds and the vertical axis is the Q of imports by the US from Britain. The demand curve is the demand for imports by the US; the supply curve is the supply of imports to the US by Britain.

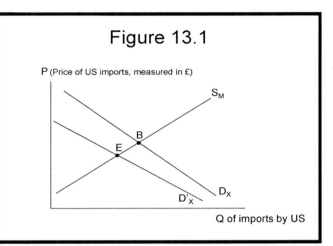

Figure 13.1

Suppose the initial equilibrium in the US import market is indicated by point B. *At point B there is some quantity of imports and some pound price. Multiplying that quantity times the price gives the number of pounds demanded by US citizens to pay for British imports.*

Now suppose there is a depreciation of the dollar. (The terms "appreciation" and "depreciation" refer to movements of the exchange rate in a floating rate system, while "**revaluation**" and "**devaluation**" are terms used to describe the infrequent changes in the exchange rate in a fixed rate system.) Because prices are measured in pounds, there will be no *direct* effect of the depreciation on British exporters, who denominate in pounds. The depreciation by itself does not change the price the British exporters receive. Thus, the import supply curve in Fig. 13.1 will not move. There is no change in the amount of goods offered by British exporters to the US.

The demand curve for imports in Fig. 13.1 will be affected by a depreciation of the dollar. With a depreciated dollar, each dollar that US importers use to buy imports from Britain will yield fewer pounds on the foreign exchange market. If US importers are to continue to purchase the same quantity of imports, the pound price they are willing to pay will have to fall by the same amount as the depreciation. Thus, the D in Fig. 13.1 will shift down by the same proportion as the depreciation of the dollar. This is shown in Fig. 13.1 by the shift from D to D'. As a consequence of the shift in the demand curve, the new equilibrium is at point E in Fig. 13.1. At point E, the pound price is lower than at point B *and* the quantity of imports is lower than at point B. Multiplying this new lower price times the new lower quantity gives a lower demand for foreign exchange than at point B. Thus, a higher dollar price of the pound produces a lower demand for pounds, as shown in Figure 13.2. In this case, the depreciation of the dollar (appreciation of the pound) leads to a decrease in the quantity demanded of pounds.

It is of some importance to note that the shape of the downward sloping demand curve for foreign exchange in Fig. 13.2 may change as the shape of the demand curve for imports in Fig. 13.1 changes. In the extreme case of a vertical demand curve for imports, depreciation will not affect the demand curve. (Shifting a vertical demand curve down leaves it unchanged.) In this extreme case, the quantity demand of foreign exchange is unchanged, so the demand curve in

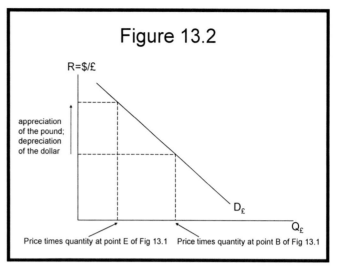

Fig. 13.2 would be vertical. Apart from this extreme case, currency depreciation will always cause the demand for foreign exchange to fall so the demand curve for foreign exchange will be downward sloping.

The market for US exports to Britain generates the supply curve of pounds in the foreign exchange market. The procedure is similar to that for generating the demand for pounds, but is different enough to warrant its own discussion. The market for US exports where the price is measured in pounds is shown in Figure 13.3. The supply curve represents the decisions of US exporters selling goods to Britain. The demand curve represents the decisions of British importers buying goods from the US. Given a price in pounds, depreciation of the dollar will not affect the British quantity demanded for US exports, so the demand curve for US exports is unchanged. US exporters, however, will be willing to export more for a given pound price

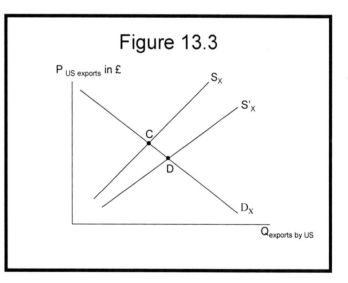

because a depreciation of the dollar will make the pound worth more dollars. For a given level of exports, US exporters will be willing to accept a lower pound price by the same proportionate amount as the depreciation. Thus, the supply of exports shifts vertically down by the same proportionate amount as the depreciation. In Fig. 13.3, a depreciation of the dollar causes equilibrium to move from point C to point D.

Notice that depreciation has an ambiguous effect on the amount of pounds that Britain will supply in order to buy US exports. The price in pounds of exports has fallen, but the quantity has decreased. If the demand curve is relatively flat —highly elastic— then the export price decrease will be small and the export quantity increase will be large. In this case, more total pounds will be supplied and depreciation will produce an increased quantity supplied of pounds. The supply curve of foreign exchange will be upward sloping. If, however, the demand curve is vertical (highly inelastic), then the price of exports will fall considerably with little change in quantity. The price multiplied by quantity will actually be lower and depreciation will cause fewer pounds to be supplied. In this case, the supply curve for foreign exchange is downward sloping! In general, the greater the elasticity of demand for exports, the more likely is the supply curve to be upward sloping. (Review this point again until it is clear.)

The above analysis of depreciation was conducted in pound prices in order to determine the effect of dollar depreciation on the quantity supplied and quantity demanded of pounds in the foreign exchange market. The analysis could also be conducted in terms of dollar prices. The results of that analysis would show that the dollar prices of US imports and exports increase. A depreciation of the dollar will increase the demand for US exports, causing the price of export goods to increase, while the supply of imports in dollars would decrease, causing the price of imports to increase. A higher price for imports would cause a substitution into import competing goods, which causes a general rise in prices in the US economy. A depreciation of the dollar will be inflationary.

Because depreciation increases the price of exports and imports, depreciation may also affect the terms of trade (the price of exports relative to the price of imports) if, as is likely, the price of exports increases by a different amount than the price of imports.

It was concluded above that the demand curve for foreign exchange will tend to be downward sloping, but the supply curve may be upward sloping or downward sloping. This leads to the possibility of a very interesting and problematic situation. Suppose in Fig. 13.3 that the demand curve for exports is very steep. Depreciation will shift down the supply curve of exports, as shown in Fig. 13.3, but with a very steep demand curve for exports, the price will fall and the quantity will not change much. Britain will need *less* total pounds to buy US exports. This, as discussed, will produce a downward sloping supply curve. Suppose it looks like that shown in Figure 13.4. Now suppose the current exchange rate is R_1, at which there is a US balance of payments deficit, because the quantity

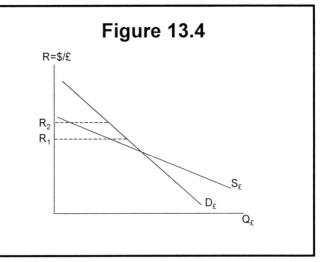

Figure 13.4

demand of foreign exchange exceeds the quantity supplied. The excess demand for foreign exchange will cause R to increase, say to R_2 (a depreciation of the dollar), which will cause an even *larger* excess demand for pounds. In this case, depreciation does not work to narrow a balance of payments deficit; it *widens the balance of payments deficit* (creates an even larger excess demand for pounds). This is an **unstable foreign exchange market**, in that a change in the exchange rate does not produce a movement towards equilibrium, but a movement away from it.

If the demand curve is downward sloping and the supply curve is upward sloping, then a disequilibrium foreign exchange rate will cause the exchange rate to move towards equilibrium. This is a **stable foreign exchange market.**

As explained above, the slope of the supply curve (upward versus downward, as well as how steep) depends upon the price elasticity of demand for exports, and the steepness of the downward sloping demand curve depends upon the price elasticity of the demand for imports. Without proof, the foreign exchange market will be stable if the sum of the price elasticities of demand for US exports and imports exceed 1.0. This is known as the **Marshall-Lerner Condition.**

Some early (1940s) estimates of elasticities suggested that the sum of the price elasticities of demand were less than or close to 1.0. Such **elasticity pessimism** casts doubt on the ability of a floating exchange rate system to correct balance of payments disequilibria. Subsequent research, however, verifies that the Marshall-Lerner condition is indeed met. Movements of the exchange rate do serve to eliminate balance of payments disequilibria.

Part of the source of elasticity pessimism resulted from looking at time periods too short to capture the full effect of exchange rate changes. In the short run, price elasticities are very small because producers and consumers adjust their plans somewhat slowly to price changes. This produces, in the very short run, an unstable foreign exchange market. A country whose currency depreciates in response to a balance of payments deficit will find itself with a larger deficit and further depreciation, until consumers and producers respond. Only in time will the deficit improve in response to the depreciation. The time path of the deficit will appear as in Figure 13.5. This phenomenon is known as the **J–curve effect**, named after the time path that the deficit produces after the depreciation.

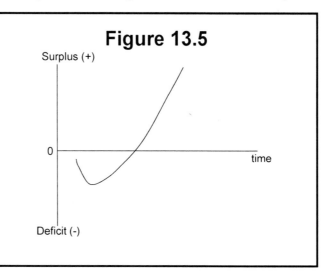

Figure 13.5

Surplus (+)

0

time

Deficit (-)

In addition to the low price elasticities of demand in the short-run, depreciation may not be effective due to a less than 100% currency **pass-through effect**. If the dollar depreciates by, say, 5% that means an automatic increase in the price of imported goods, if the home currency prices of imported goods are not changed. Foreign exporters, however, may be reluctant to allow the depreciation to increase the dollar prices charged to US buyers for fear of losing hard-earned market share. If foreign firms lower their prices, then the prices faced by US importers may not change at all.

If the exchange is held fixed, then it is the price of goods that will adjust to external surpluses and deficits. In a fixed exchange rate system, the **rules of the game** are to support the value of your currency relative to other currencies, or in the gold standard, relative to gold. If a nation experiences a balance of payments deficit, then there will be downward pressure on its exchange rate. In order to comply with the rules of the game, the central bank is obligated to support its currency by buying it with foreign currency. When a central bank buys its own currency, it is taking domestic money out of circulation. This reduction in the money supply will cause domestic prices to fall, which will stimulate exports and discourage now relatively higher priced imports, thus correcting the balance of payments deficit.

In a **gold standard**, countries agree to maintain the price of its currency relative to gold. The agreed upon gold prices implies an exchange rate between currencies. If in the United States the price of an ounce of gold is $5, and in Britain it is £1, then the implied dollar cost of the pound is $5/£1. If, on the foreign exchange market, the dollar threatens to fall due to a balance of payments deficit, then gold would be shipped between countries. For example, if on the foreign exchange market the value of the pound crept to $5.10, then no one would buy pounds directly with dollars. Gold could be purchased in the United States for $5 and shipped to Britain where it would yield £1. Gold shipments do have transaction costs, so gold would be shipped only if the foreign exchange price differed from the gold prices by an amount greater than the transaction costs. The foreign exchange prices at which gold would be shipped are called the **gold points (gold export point and gold import point)**. A deficit country would experience and outflow of gold. With gold as the money supply, or gold-backed paper, a reduction in gold means a decrease in the money supply and a reduction in goods prices. With lower goods prices, the deficit would be corrected. This movement of gold and prices is called the **price-specie-flow mechanism** and was stated by Hume in the eighteenth century to point out the mercantilist folly of attempting to produce continual balance of payments surpluses. In a fixed exchange rate system, as long as central banks agree to maintain the exchange rate, or equivalently the domestic price of gold, deficits and surpluses are eliminated automatically.

Income Adjustments in an Open Economy
In considering how prices (exchange rates and goods' prices) adjust to external deficits and surpluses, income was implicitly assumed to be unchanging in order to focus on the effect of price changes. The following focuses on income adjustments.

Income Determination in a Closed Economy
In a **closed economy** (no international transactions), with no government sector, equilibrium national income occurs when production equals spending, i.e., when

$$Y = C + I \qquad (1)$$

Y=national income or output (GDP), C=desired spending by consumers, and I=desired investment spending by firms. If Y exceeds C+I, then production exceeds spending, causing inventory accumulation, to which producers respond by lowering production (prices are assumed constant). If Y is less than C+I, then production is less than spending, so inventories will decline. Producers respond to decreases in inventories by increasing production. Only when production equals spending, Y = C + I, will income be in equilibrium.

It is assumed that investment spending, I, is given exogenously, but C depends upon the level of income. The relationship between consumption and income is called the **"consumption function"**. A linear consumption function is

$$C = a + bY \qquad (2)$$

The letters a and b constants. As income changes, C changes by b times the change in income. For example, if a = 100 and b = .8, then C = 100 + .8Y. If Y increases by 100, then C increases by 80. Algebraically, $\Delta C = .8\Delta Y$, or $\Delta C/\Delta Y = .8$. This ratio of increased consumption to increased income is called the **marginal propensity to consume (MPC)**. The MPC in equation (2) is the constant b.

Equilibrium can also be written in terms of saving and investment. Rearranging equation (1),

$$Y - C = I$$

The difference between income (Y) and consumption (C) is just saving, so equilibrium also occurs where

$$S = I$$

Like consumption, saving increases with income. The ratio of changes in savings to changes in income, $\Delta S/\Delta Y$, is the **marginal propensity to save (MPS)**. An increase in income must be saved or spent, so MPC+MPS = 1.

Because consumption depends upon income, a change in investment will lead to a larger change in income because of induced consumption. If investment spending increases by 100, then producers will respond by increasing production to meet the new demand. The receipt of the 100 by producers will be paid out as income (e.g., wages and profits), which will generate (induce) more consumption (by the MPC times the change in income), which will generate more production, and the cycle continues.

The total effect can be found by substituting C = a + bY into Y = C + I to produce

$$Y = a + bY + I$$

Solving for Y,

$$Y = [a+I]/(1-b) \tag{3}$$

Now if I increases while a is held constant, then

$$\Delta Y = \Delta I/(1-b) = \Delta I[1/(1-b)] \tag{4}$$

If ΔI = 100, and b = .8, then ΔY = 100[1/(1-.8)] = 100[5] = 500. An increase in investment spending of 100 leads to an increase in income (output) of 500. This multiplier effect is due to the effect of increased income on consumption, which increases income, etc., as explained above. The **multiplier** in this case is 5, which is equal to [1/(1-b)]. Because the MPC and the MPS must add to one, equation (4) can be written as

$$\Delta Y = \Delta I[1/MPS]$$

Notice that variables a and I enter equation (3) in the same way. An increase in the variable a will have the same multiplier effect on income as an increase in variable I. Variable a can be interpreted as those things that affect consumption other than income.

Income Determination in an Open Economy

With this brief review of the principles of income determination in a closed economy, we can now add the external sector, consisting of exports and imports (capital flows are not part of the analysis). Consumption (C) is total consumption by domestics, so in an open economy it includes consumption of both domestic and foreign goods. To get domestic spending imports must be subtracted. The value of exports is the value of spending on domestic goods by foreigners. In an open economy, then, total spending on domestic goods is C + I + X - M, where X is exports and M is imports. Domestic income will be in equilibrium when

$$Y = C + I + X - M \qquad (5)$$

Equilibrium can written in an alternative way by subtracting C from both sides of equation (5) to produce

$$Y - C = I + X - M$$

The difference between Y and C is just savings, so

$$S = I + X - M, \text{ or}$$

$$S + M = I + X$$

This is an expression of equilibrium using the leakages-injections approach. In the absence of trade, the only leakage from spending is saving and the only injection is investment. Thus, in a closed economy, equilibrium occurs where S = I. In an open economy, imports represent an additional leakage from spending and exports represent an additional injection. (With a government sector another leakage would be taxes and another injection would be government spending.)

It is assumed that exports, like investment, do not depend upon domestic income. Imports, however, do depend on domestic income in much the same way that total consumption depends upon domestic income. As domestic income increases, imports will increase. If the relationship is linear, then the **import function** can be written as

$$M = c + dY$$

The letters c and d are constants. As income increases, imports increase by d, or $\Delta M = d\Delta Y$, or $\Delta M / \Delta Y = d$. The constant d is the **marginal propensity to import (MPM)**, and represents the fraction of an *increase* in income that is spent on imports. Notice that the MPM is *not* the fraction of income that goes towards imports, but the fraction of an *increase* in income that goes towards imports. The fraction of income that goes towards imports is M/Y, and is called the **average propensity to import (APM)**.

In an open economy, imports will influence the size of the multiplier. If investment increases, then production will increase as firms satisfy the new spending. They will receive that as income and consume some fraction, and the process will continue. However, in an open economy, some income leaks out into imports. Thus the presence of imports will change the multiplier. To derive the multiplier, first write out equilibrium as

$$Y = C + I + X - M.$$

Now using $C = a + bY$, and $M = c + dY$,

$$Y = a + bY + I + X - (c + dY).$$

Solving for Y produces

$$Y = [a + I + X]/(1-b+d). \qquad (6)$$

Now if I increases while a and X are held constant, the change in Y will be

$$\Delta Y = \Delta I/(1-b+d) = \Delta I[1/(1-b+d)].$$

The multiplier is now $[1/(1-b+d)]$. Letting $b = .8$ and $d = .3$ (recall that the b = MPC is a fraction and d = MPM is a fraction), the multiplier is $[1/(1-.8+.3)] = 2$. If there were no imports ($d=0$), then the multiplier would be $[1/(1-.8+0)] = 5$. Imports serve to reduce the size of the multiplier because some of the increased spending "leaks" abroad in the form of spending on imports. Notice that the variable X enters equation (6) in the same way that variables a and I do, so they will all be subject to same multiplier effect. Summarizing:

$$\Delta Y = \Delta I[1/(1-b+d)] \quad \text{(if X and a do not change)},$$
$$\Delta Y = \Delta a[1/(1-b+d)] \quad \text{(if X and I do not change), and}$$
$$\Delta Y = \Delta X[1/(1-b+d)] \quad \text{(if a and I do not change)}.$$

The above multipliers for changes in a, I, and X assume a small country. If the country is large then any changes in the domestic economy will affect its trading partners and produce **foreign repercussions**. If, for example, domestic investment increases in the United States, then US income will increase by the multiplier effect. Along with the increase in US income will be an increase in US imports. Thus, exports of foreign countries will increase, which will increase foreign income. When foreign incomes are higher, foreigners will import more from the United States, which will increase US exports. This will now further increase US income and the cycle, although smaller at each step in the process, continues. The presence of foreign repercussions will increase the size of the multiplier.

This is one way in which economic activity is transmitted between countries. A business expansion in Europe will produce an expansion in the United States, which will reinforce the expansion in Europe, etc. The process also works in reverse. A recession in Europe can produce a recession in the United States, which will aggravate the recession in Europe, etc.

Given the relationship between trade and income just described, we can begin a synthesis of price adjustments and income adjustments. We saw that currency depreciation (or devaluation in a fixed exchange rate system) would improve the trade balance if the Marshall-Lerner condition for elasticities were met. However, when income adjustments and the level of economic activity are introduced, the process is more complex. First, an improvement in the trade balance (X-M) due to depreciation will increase domestic income because it means an increase in exports relative to imports - an increase in spending on domestic income. If domestic income increases, this generates an increase in imports, offsetting some of that improvement. Second, the trade balance can improve only if income is below its full employment level. If income is at full employment, then an increase in X-M will only cause prices to increase, which will make an economy less competitive relative to its trading partners, reversing the correction of the deficit.

The importance of the level of economic activity is emphasized by the **absorption approach** to adjustment. The absorption approach begins with the equilibrium condition for income:

$$Y = C + I + X - M.$$

Domestic absorption is total spending by domestics (the value of goods absorbed by the domestic economy), and so is equal to C + I. Let absorption A = C+ I. Substituting this into the equilibrium condition and solving for the trade balance produces

$$X - M = Y - A.$$

The absorption approach emphasizes the arguments made above about the effectiveness of depreciation (devaluation) in correcting a trade deficit. The trade balance (X-M) can increase only if Y increases relative to A. If Y is at less than full employment, then currency depreciation will increase Y because it will increase spending on domestic goods by both foreigners and domestics. (Depreciation of a country's currency makes domestic goods cheaper to foreigners and makes foreign goods more expensive to domestics. Depreciation "switches" demand from foreign to domestic goods.) As Y increases, it also increases consumption, which is part of A. Thus, depreciation increases Y and A, and will only improve the trade balance if Y increases faster than A.

If Y is at full employment, then Y cannot increase so depreciation will work only if it decreases A. Absorption can fall with currency depreciation if the depreciation redistributes income to those who spend less, or if the price increases due to depreciation reduce wealth. The absorption approach suggests that depreciation may have to be accompanied by other domestic policies (fiscal and/or monetary) that will directly reduce A.

The income adjustments described assume that the exchange rate could change. If exchange rates are fixed, then the adjustment is different. With fixed exchange rates, a deficit will initially put downward pressure on a country's exchange rate, to which the central bank will have to respond by buying its own currency with foreign exchange reserves. This reduces the domestic money supply, which has a number of effects. First, less money will reduce prices relative to trading partners, which will improve the trade balance, as in the price-specie-flow mechanism. Second, less money will contract income, which will reduce imports, which improves the trade balance. Finally, less money increases interest rates, which attracts foreign capital, allowing a nation to finance its deficit by borrowing from abroad. Capital inflows, to this point, have not been included in the analysis, but adjustments to trade deficits often occur through an inflow of capital rather than an elimination of the trade deficit.

Synthesis of Income and Price Adjustments

A brief summary of the adjustment mechanisms is in order. In a flexible exchange rate system, a deficit will cause a depreciation of a country's currency. The absorption approach points out that this may not work if the economy is at full employment, because it will only translate into price increases that will restore the deficit. If there is less than full employment, then currency depreciation will also increase domestic absorption, which will partially offset the improvement in the deficit, requiring a larger depreciation. The cost to a country of relying on changes in the value of its currency includes foreign exchange risk as well as the very real costs associated with continually expanding and contracting export and import-competing sectors.

In a fixed rate system a deficit leads to monetary contraction, a fall in prices and income, and an increase in interest rates. A fixed exchange rate means giving up control of the money supply in order to maintain the fixed exchange rate.

Because of the costs associated with adjustment under both types of exchange rate systems, as well as the dubious effectiveness of adjustment under flexible exchange rates, countries have often resorted to discretionary policies (fiscal and monetary policies) to supplant or replace the automatic adjustments.

Key Terms used in Chapter Summary and Review
(The list below is not necessarily the same as the list provided by the Salvatore text.)

Absorption approach

Average propensity to import (APM)

Closed economy

Consumption function

Devaluation

Elasticity pessimism

Foreign repercussions

Gold Standard

Gold points

Import function

J–curve effect

Marginal propensity to consume (MPC)

Marginal propensity to import (MPM)

Marginal propensity to save (MPS)

Marshall-Lerner Condition

Multiplier

Pass-through effect

Price-specie-flow mechanism

Revaluation

Rules of the game

Stable foreign exchange market

Unstable foreign exchange market

Multiple Choice Questions

1. As a result of a depreciation of the dollar relative to the Euro, the equilibrium Euro price of US imports will
a) Increase and the quantity of imports will increase.
b) Decrease and the equilibrium quantity of imports will decrease.
c) Increase and the equilibrium quantity of imports will decrease.
d) Decrease and the equilibrium quantity of imports will increase.

2. If the foreign exchange market is unstable then a depreciation of the US dollar
a) Can be described by the Marshall-Lerner condition.
b) Will not reduce a trade deficit.
c) Will not affect the value of exports and imports.
d) Will be reversed.

3. The J-curve occurs because in the short run
a) Price elasticities are low.
b) The Marshall-Lerner condition is met.
c) The foreign exchange market is stable.
d) Currency pass-through is 100%.

4. In a fixed exchange rate system, which of the following will occur as a result of a US trade deficit?
a) Depreciation of the US dollar.
b) Appreciation of the US dollar.
c) An increase in the US money supply.
d) A decrease in the US money supply.

5. Prior to depreciation of the dollar the average price of US exports was 50 Euros and the quantity of US exports was 100. After depreciation of the dollar the average price of US exports is 60 and the quantity of US exports is 80. Based on these prices and quantities, which of the following is true?
a) The demand curve for Euros is upward sloping.
b) The supply curve of Euros is downward sloping.
c) The Marshall-Lerner condition is met.
d) There can't be a J-curve.

6. Relative to a closed economy an open economy is most likely to have which of the following?
a) Fewer kinds of leakages.
b) Fewer kinds of injections.
c) A lower multiplier.
d) Greater foreign repercussions.

7. If European income increases, leading to an increase in imports from Japan, which of the following is likely?
a) Income will fall in Japan.
b) The Japanese yen will depreciate if the yen floats.
c) The Japanese money supply will fall if the yen is fixed.
d) Japanese spending will increase by more than the increase in European imports.

8. A depreciation will not be effective if
a) The Marshall-Lerner condition is met.
b) The foreign exchange market is stable.
c) Income increases more than absorption.
d) Absorption increases and income is unchanged.

9. A trade deficit will reduce the money supply
a) In a flexible exchange rate system.
b) In a gold standard.
c) If absorption falls.
d) If prices fall.

10. In a fixed exchange rate system, a deficit is automatically corrected through
a) A decreases in absorption.
b) A decrease in income and prices.
c) An increase in income and a decrease in prices.
d) A decrease in income and an increase in prices.

Problems and Discussion Questions

1. Why is an economy in which inflation is a significant problem less likely to use depreciation alone as a way of eliminating a balance of payments deficit?

2. a) What causes gold to move between countries in a gold standard, in which each country agrees to maintain the domestic price of gold?

b) How do economies adjust to balance of payments disequilibria in a gold standard?

3. Each of the graphs below shows the effect of a depreciation of the dollar relative to the pound. In each case, draw the accompanying supply and demand curves for foreign exchange, and determine whether the foreign exchange market is stable or unstable.

a)

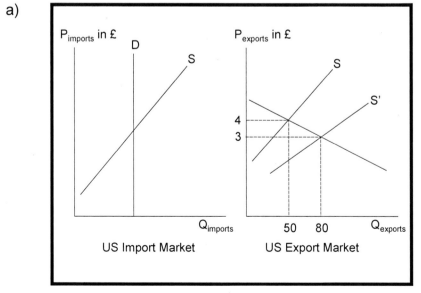

b)

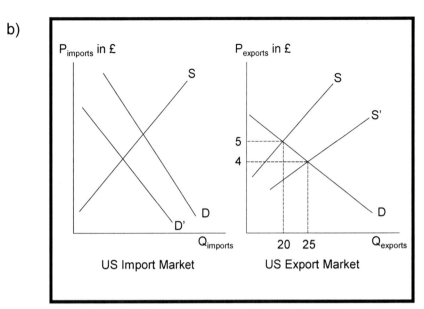

US Import Market   US Export Market

c)

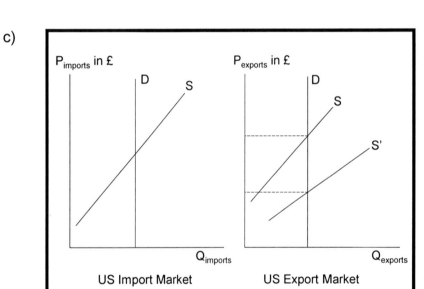

US Import Market   US Export Market

4. Of the three cases in Question 3, which case best explains the early part of the J-curve phenomenon, in which depreciation actually causes a deterioration of the balance of payments? Explain.

5. Suppose the components of spending in an economy are as follows.

C = 100 + .75Y   M = 50 + .25Y
I = 400   X = 300

a) What is the equilibrium level of income?

b) What is the trade balance (X-M) at this equilibrium?

c) Suppose exports increase by 100. What is the new equilibrium level of income?

d) What is the trade balance (X-M) at the new equilibrium? Did the trade balance improve by the increase in exports of 100? Explain.

6. a) Suppose Kenya is currently experiencing full employment, has a fixed exchange rate relative to its major trading partners, and exports currently equal imports. If the economies of Kenya's trading partners experience a severe recession, explain the automatic adjustments that will take place in Kenya. Include a discussion of Kenya's exports, imports (and import-competing sectors), money supply, income, price level, interest rates and international capital flows. (Ignore repercussion effects.)

b) Why might Kenya be reluctant to allow the automatic adjustments to take place?

Chapter 14
Adjustment Policies

Chapter Outline

Chapter Summary and Review

The automatic adjustment policies described in Chapter 13 can have some costly side effects. With fixed exchange rates a deficit will produce monetary contraction as the domestic currency is purchased with foreign exchange reserves by the monetary authorities. This decrease in the money supply produces falling prices and incomes. With floating exchange rates a deficit will produce depreciation, which, if effective, will shift resources to the export sectors. Labor and other factors will bear the costs of that transition. In addition, the depreciation may produce inflation as both domestic and foreign residents switch demand to domestic goods.

External Balance and Internal Balance

Internal balance is defined as full employment with price stability. **External balance** is defined as balance of payments equilibrium, which will initially mean equality of exports and imports until capital flows are introduced. Because adjustment to external imbalances may be costly and may not be compatible with full employment, governments may wish to adopt adjustment policies to support or offset the automatic adjustments discussed in Chapter 13. Government has a number of adjustment policies to influence employment and the balance of payments. These policies can be classified as **expenditure–changing policies**, **expenditure–switching policies**, and **direct controls**.

Expenditure-changing polices are those that change the general level of economic activity by changing aggregate demand. Expenditure-changing policies include fiscal and monetary policies. Fiscal policy is the use of the spending and taxing functions of government. An expansionary fiscal policy is one that increases aggregate demand by lowering taxes or increasing government spending. Similarly, a contractionary fiscal policy is one that reduces aggregate demand by increasing taxes or decreasing government spending.

Monetary policy is the control of the money supply by a nation's central bank. An expansionary monetary is one that increases the money supply. An increase in the money supply will lower interest rates, which increases borrowing for spending. The increased spending increases aggregate demand and the equilibrium level of output. Contractionary monetary policy raises the interest through reductions in the money supply. The higher interest rate lowers spending, which lowers equilibrium income.

Expenditure-changing policies affect external balance primarily by changing domestic income. An expansionary expenditure-changing policy increases domestic income, and by increasing imports, moves the balance of payments towards deficit. A contractionary expenditure-changing policy, through the same channels, moves the balance of payments towards surplus.

An expenditure-switching policy is a change in the exchange rate. If a nation's currency depreciates, domestic goods become cheaper to foreign residents, and foreign goods become more expensive to domestic residents. Both domestic and foreign residents respond by switching some expenditures to the nation whose currency has depreciated. By increasing domestic spending, currency depreciation will also offset some of its own effects on the trade balance because some of the increased spending goes to imports.

Direct controls are also expenditure-switching policies and include tariffs, quotas, exchange controls, and wage and price controls. In general, direct controls work by controlling imports or exports.

Adjustment Policies with Fixed but Changeable Exchange Rates

T.W. Swan developed a model of how policy might be used to achieve simultaneous external and external balance. Although the model was quite simple, it did reveal an important point. A policy aimed at achieving internal balance may create or worsen external imbalance and vice versa. As an example, suppose an economy is at full employment with a trade deficit. If policymakers devalue the currency, then the external balance may improve, but the switch in demand to domestic goods may cause inflation.

As another example, suppose an economy has a deficit and unemployment. An increase in government spending to produce full employment will increase incomes and increase imports, so the deficit will worsen.

The lesson of Swan's analysis, as stated more generally by the economist J. Tinbergen, is that the number of objectives must be no greater than the number of policy instruments to achieve those objectives. If external and internal balances are objectives, then there must be at least two policy instruments. To achieve internal and external balance a nation will have to use both and expenditure-changing policy and an expenditure-switching policy.

Nations often resist changing their currency in a fixed exchange rate system for a number of reasons. A change in the exchange rate does entail a significant reallocation of resources towards export sectors, which can be costly to the participants. In addition, many nations may find their currency's value to be a source of national pride and avoid depreciation. Where there is reluctance to use an expenditure changing policy like the exchange rate, a nation is left with expenditure-changing policies.

Expenditure-Changing Policies Under Fixed Rates

Another name for expenditure-changing polices is demand-management policies because they work by changing aggregate demand. The traditional and accepted policies to change aggregate demand are monetary and fiscal policies. An important element of the effect of monetary and fiscal policies is the effect of such policies on the interest rate.

Monetary Policy Under Fixed Rates

An increase in the money supply will expand output by decreasing interest rates and stimulating investment and other interest-sensitive components of spending (such as consumption). With a fixed exchange rate, there is a constraint on monetary policy. First, the higher income increases imports, which puts downward pressure on the nation's currency (upward pressure on foreign currency). In addition, when international capital movements are highly mobile, the lower interest rate produced by the increase in the money supply leads to capital outflow as investors seek higher returns abroad. This also puts downward pressure on the nation's currency. In order to keep the exchange rate fixed, the monetary authorities must buy their own currency with foreign reserves. Buying the domestic currency reduces the nation's money supply. The attempt to increase the money supply leads to a decrease in the money supply. In order to keep the exchange rate at its fixed level, the interest rate must return to its original level. This means the money supply will be unchanged. With a fixed exchange rate, a nation has no control over its money supply. In the long run the money supply must be consistent with the exchange rate. The money supply is tied to the exchange rate, so monetary policy is used to achieve external balance.

Fiscal Policy Under Fixed Rates

Unlike monetary policy, fiscal policy is effective under fixed exchange rates. If government spending increases then income and output will expand by the multiplier. The expansion in income increases imports so the external balance deteriorates but the fiscal expansion also increases interest rates as the government borrows to finance the increase in government spending. If capital is highly responsive to interest rates, then the inflow of capital will be large and the internal balance improves, despite the increased imports. The upward pressure on the nation's economy means the monetary authority will have to sell its currency to keep the exchange rate fixed which increases the money supply. The increased money supply lowers interest rates and provides for further expansion. With a fixed exchange rate expansionary fiscal policy is effective in changing income and output because it also leads to an increase in the money supply.

Policy Mix Under Fixed Rates

With fixed exchange rates money is committed to maintaining the exchange rate, so it is effective in achieving external balance, but it is not effective in achieving internal balance. Fiscal policy can influence internal balance and external balance, but as explained above, one policy may not always be able to achieve two objectives. Nobel prize winner Robert Mundell developed the **assignment rule** based on relative effectiveness (comparative advantage?) of the two policies. Monetary policy's effectiveness is in reaching external balance if exchange rates are fixed, so in a fixed exchange rate system, *assign monetary policy to external balance and fiscal policy to internal balance.*

As an example, assume a nation faces an external deficit and a recession, which it chooses to address with adjustment policies. According to Mundell's assignment rule, monetary policy should be directed to the deficit and fiscal policy to the recession. Fiscal policy, directed at the recession should be expansionary. Expansionary policy will also increase interest rates, attracting capital, which will help with the external deficit. It is unlikely that the size of the fiscal expansion needed to reach each balance is exactly the same, so monetary policy, with no effect on income in a fixed rate system, can address any remaining external imbalance.

Expenditure-Changing Policies Under Flexible Exchange Rates

With fixed exchange rates, monetary policy is ineffective and fiscal policy is effective. With flexible exchange rates, policy effectiveness is reversed. Fiscal policy becomes ineffective and monetary policy becomes effective in changing domestic income and output. The external balance is not an issue with flexible rates because market forces move the rate to where there is external balance.

Monetary Policy

An increase in the money supply will lower interest rates, stimulate investment and increase aggregate demand. The lower interest rates will also cause a capital outflow, leading to a depreciation of the exchange rate. The depreciation of the exchange rates increases net exports (increases exports and reduces imports), which also increases aggregate demand. With flexible exchange rates monetary policy is effective in changing the level of income and output.

Fiscal Policy

An increase in government spending, financed with borrowing will lead to an increase in interest rates. Although the increased spending will lead to greater imports, the effect of the interest rates on capital inflows will be very large if capital is mobile. The inflow of capital will appreciate the exchange rate, which will reduce net exports (reduce exports and increase imports), which will offset the expansionary effect of the fiscal policy. Fiscal policy tends to be ineffective in a flexible exchange rate system.

Key Terms used in Chapter Summary and Review
(The list below is not necessarily the same as the list provided by the Salvatore text.)

Internal balance

Expenditure–switching policies

External balance

Direct controls

Expenditure–changing policies

Assignment rule

Multiple Choice Questions

1. Suppose a nation has met the objective of external balance, but not the objective of internal balance. Which of the following is true?
a) Internal balance cannot be produced by the use of two instruments.
b) The use of only one instrument is necessary.
c) The use of two instruments is necessary.
d) Both objectives cannot be reached.

2. A nation's expenditure-changing policies work primarily by
a) Changing spending in both the foreign and domestic economy.
b) Shifting spending between economies.
c) Changing spending within the nation.
d) Changing the exchange rate.

3. A nation's expenditure-switching policies work primarily by
a) Changing fiscal policy
b) Shifting spending between economies.
c) Managing the money supply.
d) Changing the exchange rate.

4. Which of the following is an example of an expenditure-switching policy?
a) Fiscal policy.
b) Monetary policy.
c) Interest-rate policy.
d) Currency revaluation.

5. With fixed exchange rates and very mobile international capital movements, monetary policy is
a) An effective expenditure switching policy.
b) An effective expenditure changing policy.
c) An ineffective expenditure changing policy.
d) Has no effect on capital movements.

6. With fixed exchange rates and highly mobile international capital movements, fiscal policy is
a) An effective expenditure switching policy.
b) An effective expenditure changing policy.
c) An ineffective expenditure changing policy.
d) Has no effect on capital movements.

7. A nation with a fixed exchange rate system has an external surplus and an internal recession. If capital is highly mobile, then
a) Monetary policy should be expansionary and fiscal policy should be expansionary.
b) Monetary policy should be expansionary and fiscal policy should be contractionary.
c) Monetary policy should be contractionary and fiscal policy should be expansionary.
d) Monetary policy should be contractionary and fiscal policy should be contractionary.

8. With flexible exchange rates and internal inflation
a) Monetary policy should be expansionary.
b) Monetary policy should be contractionary.
c) Fiscal policy should be contractionary.
d) Fiscal policy should be expansionary.

9. The US has a floating exchange rate relative to its major trading partners. In 2003 the US was moving towards internal recession. If the policy response were a major cut in federal taxes and international capital was highly mobile, then the most likely outcome would be
a) Expanding income and an increased trade deficit.
b) Unchanged income and an increased trade deficit.
c) Increased income and external balance.
d) Decreased income and external surplus.

10. Europe has flexible exchange rates with respect to its major trading partners. If Europe attempts to reduce inflation with monetary policy then
a) It must also use contractionary fiscal policy.
b) It must also use expansionary fiscal policy.
c) It will be successful in reducing inflation.
d) It will need wage-price controls.

Problems and Discussion Questions

1. According to Mundell's assignment rule, determine the direction of fiscal and monetary policy necessary to correct the following situations in a fixed exchange rate system.
a) External deficit and inflation

b) External deficit and unemployment

c) External surplus and inflation

d) External surplus and unemployment

2. What effect will contractionary fiscal policy have on the following in a fixed exchange rate system if capital is very mobile internationally?
a) The money supply.

b) Output and income.

3. What effect will expansionary monetary policy have on the following in a fixed exchange rate system?
a) The money supply.

b) Output and income.

4. With floating exchange rates, which policy, monetary or fiscal, would you suggest in the following cases? Also indicate whether the policy should be expansionary or contractionary.
a) Recession.

b) Inflation.

5. A nation on a fixed exchange rate system has been running a trade deficit for many years, which has been financed by international capital inflows. Suppose foreign investors become concerned about their investments and quickly withdraw funds. What effect will this have on the following?
a) The money supply.

b) Output and income.

6. A nation has fixed exchange rates and the income of its trading partners increases significantly. What effect will this have on the nation's
a) Money supply?

b) Output and income.

7. Explain the effect on output and income of the following in a nation with floating exchange rates and high capital mobility.
a) Contractionary monetary policy

b) Contractionary fiscal policy.

Part Six: The International Monetary System: Past, Present, and Future

Chapter 15
Flexible versus Fixed Exchange Rates, European Monetary Systems, and Macroeconomic Policy Coordination

Chapter Outline

Chapter Summary and Review

Fixed Versus Flexible Exchange Rates

This chapter discusses the relative merits and implications of alternative exchange rate systems. A **freely floating exchange-rate system,** or **clean float**, is a system in which exchange rates are allowed to continuously equate the supply and demand for foreign exchange with no government intervention in the foreign exchange market. One argument for floating exchange rates is that a freely floating rate will efficiently maintain continuous balance of payments equilibrium. In a fixed exchange rate system, external deficits and surpluses produce changes in the money supply, which create changes in internal prices of all goods and services. It is more efficient for one price -the exchange rate- to change than to change all internal prices, which may be rigid, or at least "sticky."

In a **fixed exchange-rate system**, governments must choose a particular value of the exchange rate to defend, and there is no guarantee that the correct value of the exchange rate will be chosen. If the wrong value of the exchange rate is chosen, then the goods exported and imported may not be appropriate in terms of comparative advantage. As the exchange rate changes, some goods become non-competitive internationally and others become competitive. In addition, if the exchange rate is not the equilibrium exchange rate, then there will be continuous pressure on the exchange rate to move. Added to these possible costs of a fixed exchange rate is the cost of the government bureaucracy necessary to administer the fixed exchange rate.

Additionally, in a world where there are limited policies to achieve many goals, a fixed exchange rate system removes the exchange rate as a policy tool. In a fixed exchange-rate system, exchange rates change only at discrete intervals. With a flexible exchange rate, the exchange rate can move to produce external balance, while fiscal policy and monetary policy are freed to pursue other objectives like full employment and growth.

Although the private sector may find fixed rates easier for planning and currency conversion, there are forward markets, futures markets, and options markets in foreign currency that can be used to hedge foreign currency exposure, as discussed in Chapter 11. Advocates of fixed exchange rates argue that those who favor flexible rates underestimate the risk associated with exchange rate movements. Since the adoption of floating rates among the major developed economies in the early 1970s, exchange rates have exhibited considerable volatility. Although the risk of particular transactions can be hedged with various foreign currency instruments, an entire business cannot be hedged. The decision to build a factory in Atlanta for exporting to Europe can prove unsuccessful as a result of a continued appreciation of the dollar. Hedging instruments are relatively short term, and do not allow a company to maintain a long-term comparative advantage. The reply by floating-rate advocates is that under the same kind of economic pressures that would lead to an appreciation with floating rates, fixed rates would also have to change. Those who prefer floating rates also argue that the kinds of changes that occur with fixed rates are large and abrupt, imposing as much cost as smaller, continuous changes in a floating rate.

Fixed exchange rates may impose inflationary discipline on an economy. This argument is known as the "**anchor argument**." With a fixed exchange rate, domestic inflation will lead to decreased exports and increased imports, which will put downward pressure on the exchange rate. To maintain the exchange rate the nation's monetary authority will buy domestic currency, reducing the domestic money supply and restraining inflation. If inflationary pressures repeatedly occur, there will be a loss of foreign exchange reserves that will force policy makers to curb their inflationary policies. Mexico's decision to attempt to maintain a fixed exchange rate prior to 1994 is an example of the use of an exchange rate as an inflation anchor. Flexible exchange rates impose no such anchor. With flexible rates, inflation causes a depreciation of the domestic currency, and such depreciation is in itself inflationary. Flexible rate advocates respond that with floating rates, countries can choose different rates of inflation. This is not possible with a fixed exchange because if inflation rates differ there will be pressure on the exchange rate, which will produce monetary changes. Fixed rate nations cannot pursue an independent monetary policy. Additionally, nations with fixed rates need not control inflation; they can always abandon the fixed rate, often in crisis, as in the case of the Mexican peso devaluation of 1994.

The types of disturbances faced by a country can also influence the choice of an exchange-rate system. A country with substantial external shocks will find that a floating rate insulates the domestic economy from those shocks, the shock being absorbed by changes in the exchange rate. Countries with internal shocks would find that floating rates add to instability. An internally generated expansion, for example, will increase imports, causing a currency depreciation, which would cause a larger expansion as exports increase and imports decrease in response to the depreciation. Internal expansion with fixed exchange rates would lead to a defense of the currency, which would cause monetary contraction, offsetting the expansion.

The volatility of floating exchange rates depends, in part, on the actions of speculators. If speculators are, on average, correct about the movement of the exchange rate, buying currencies when they are cheap and selling them when they are expensive, then speculation will be *stabilizing*. Stabilizing speculation occurs when the action of speculators produces a smoother time path of the exchange rate than would exist in the absence of speculation. If speculators do indeed buy low and sell high, then they will reduce swings in the exchange rate, their actions not letting exchange rates get too low nor too high. Proponents of floating rates argue that speculators cannot, on average, be wrong. If they were wrong –buying high and selling low– then they would be out of business. Floating–rate proponents argue that a fixed exchange rate is prone to crisis for it becomes apparent when there is pressure on an exchange rate to change as readily observable reserve balances used to intervene in the foreign exchange market change. With apparent pressure on the exchange rate, speculators can take relatively safe bets for and against exchange rates, and their actions will put further pressure on the exchange rate to change, resulting in major costly currency devaluations.

Advocates of fixed rates argue that a credible fixed exchange rate policy will create stabilizing speculation. If speculators believe that the monetary authority will maintain a fixed exchange rate, then they will not bet that the exchange rate will change. Indeed, as an exchange rate in a fixed-rate system reaches its announced limit (fixed exchange rates usually are allowed to move within a narrowly defined band), they will bet on its return because they believe government will act to produce its return. Speculators, then, will actually do the work of the monetary authority, stabilizing the exchange rate within the announced band.

In summary, the advantages of a floating-rate system are efficiency, policy freedom, including the decision to pursue an independent rate of inflation, and insulation from external shocks. The advantages of a fixed-rate system are reduced uncertainty, inflation control and insulation from internal disturbances.

The choice of an exchange rate system depends on the anticipated costs and benefits for the nation in question. A relatively small economy with significant exports and imports to a few large countries will find that a floating rate creates risk for a significant amount of the country's economic activities, and so will establish a fixed rate relative to their large trading partners. A large, relatively closed nation, with inflation preferences different than other nations will choose a floating exchange rate. For a relatively closed nation, a floating rate adds risk to only a small part of economic activity.

Optimum Currency Areas, Currency Boards, and Dollarization

Related to the fixed versus floating exchange–rate debate is the theory of **optimum currency areas**. A fixed exchange rate is one in which participating nations attempt to maintain a given exchange rate, with currency devaluations pursued only when pressures on the given exchange rate are large and unlikely to be reversed. An optimum currency area, on the other hand, is one in within which it is optimal for exchange rates to be permanently fixed. The United States is a currency area (not necessarily an optimum one) in which a dollar in Boston is always equivalent to a dollar in Hartford, or in New York, or in Phoenix. The benefit of a one-currency area is the certainty of exchange and the reduced costs associated with changing money. With flexible exchange rates between many regions of the United States, the size of the market would be limited. Each region would turn inward, avoiding, to some degree, the risk of external transactions. The benefits of trade, including the usual comparative advantage benefits, as well as the economies of scale benefits, would be reduced.

The disadvantage of a currency area is that each region in the currency area does not possess a separate monetary policy. Each region uses the same money and so is subject to the same monetary policy. If one region is experiencing unemployment, then it must rely on the redistributive policies of the central policy maker and the ability of labor to migrate from depressed regions to expanding regions. *A currency area is more desirable the more similar are preferences towards the rate of inflation and the greater the mobility of resources among regions.*

Similar to, but stopping just short of a currency area, is a **currency board arrangement**. A currency board arrangement is a fixed exchange rate system where the monetary authority relinquishes control of monetary policy. A fixed exchange rate is announced usually relative to one anchor currency, or some weighted average of currencies. In order to establish the credibility of the fixed exchange rate, the new rate is often part of the laws governing the operation of the currency board. The currency board takes a completely passive stance with respect to monetary policy. The board is required to maintain the exchange rate and can accumulate no assets other than the reserves of the anchor currency.

If there is a surplus relative to the anchor currency, then the nation's exchange rate will threaten to appreciate, to which the currency board will respond by buying the anchor currency, expanding the money supply. If there is a deficit then the currency will threaten to depreciate, to which the currency board will respond by buying its currency with the anchor currency's reserves. Thus, monetary expansion will only occur when reserves of the anchor currency increase and monetary contraction will only occur when reserves of the anchor currency decrease.

Because the currency board can accumulate no assets other than reserves of the anchor currency, inflation as well as interest rates will mimic that of the anchor currency. Inflation in the anchor currency will spill over as a surplus in the nation with the currency board and cause inflation. It is, therefore, important to choose an anchor currency with stable inflation.

The commitment to a currency board is a strong commitment to produce inflation rates equal to those of the anchor currency. To the extent that the commitment is credible, the currency board will be able to reduce inflationary expectations, which is instrumental in reducing actual inflation and interest rates.

Because a credible commitment to a stable inflation is important in establishing stable inflation, some nations may go further than a currency boards and actually adopt the currency of a stable nation. Because many nations (e.g. Ecuador, El Salvador, and Panama) have adopted the dollar as their own currency, the practice is called **dollarization**, although any currency could be adopted. Dollarization has benefits and costs similar to those of any fixed exchange-rate system, but is more likely to be realized because it is a more complete commitment and so less likely to be reversed.

The Euro

Europe is an example of an area that decided to move away from exchange-rate flexibility and towards, first, relatively fixed rates, and then a single currency. In 1979 the **European Monetary System** was established in which relatively fixed rates were established among members. The experiment culminated in the establishment of the **Euro** in 1999 in which all members adopted the euro as their common currency. In order to be part of the one-currency area, each participating nation was required to meet certain economic convergence criteria as established by the **Maastricht Treaty**. These convergence criteria included limits on inflation rates, budget deficits, interest rates and exchange rate fluctuations. The purpose of the convergence criteria was to attempt to create similar monetary conditions in each future member of the Euro area. With one currency, no nation can pursue an independent monetary policy, so the monetary conditions must be aligned among all member nations.

It is expected that one currency will save considerable resources involved in currency conversions, reduce inflation, and reduce the risks of trade and investment between European countries. The cost is the loss of control over their money supply that each member nation gives up to the European Central Bank.

Exchange Rate Systems

Exchange-rate systems have been referred to as fixed or flexible (floating). In practice, these systems represent polar extremes of possible exchange-rate systems. Other than in single currency areas, a fixed exchange-rate system is usually one in which a par value is established for the exchange rate, but the exchange rate is allowed to move within a relatively narrow band around par. Within the band the exchange rate can move according to the supply and demand for foreign exchange, but is restricted to the band by government intervention. For example, the Bretton Woods system allowed fluctuations within 1% of an agreed upon dollar par value, and in the gold system the gold points determined the band.

An **adjustable peg system** is equivalent to the band version of fixed exchange rates, but it is recognized that the par value may have to be changed. The difficulty, of course, is for participants in the system to agree as to when a new par should be established. The issue is one of determining whether pressures on the exchange rate are permanent, requiring a change in the par value, or temporary, in which case the par value should not be changed.

A **crawling peg system**, or **gliding parity**, is an adjustable–peg system in which a new par value is established in announced increments rather than all at once. If a nation has an inflation rate in excess of its trading partners, then a new par value will have to be established continuously. A crawling peg allows an orderly way of continuously changing the exchange rate while maintaining some of the benefits of a fixed-rate system.

Finally, a **managed floating exchange–rate system** or **dirty float** is one in which the exchange rate is allowed to be determined by market forces in the long run, but the monetary authority attempts to smooth the short-run fluctuations. If it is assumed that there are short-run cycles within long-run changes in the exchange rate, then the monetary authority can reduce some short-run fluctuations -**leaning against the wind**-by selling a small amount of domestic currency on the foreign exchange market when the exchange rate appreciates, and by buying a small amount when the exchange rate depreciates.

Whatever exchange rate system is adopted, it has to be recognized that economic conditions in one country will affect those in other countries. This issue has become particularly acute because the proportion of economic activity accounted for by international transactions has increased. Because good policy in one nation could be bad for another nation, **international macroeconomic policy coordination** is beneficial, but examples of well-planned policy coordination are few.

Key Terms used in Chapter Summary and Review

(The list below is not necessarily the same as the list provided by the Salvatore text.)

Adjustable peg system

Anchor argument

Clean float

Crawling peg system

Currency board arrangement

Dirty float

Dollarization

Euro

European Monetary System

Fixed exchange-rate system

Freely floating exchange-rate system

Gliding parity

International macroeconomic policy
    coordination

Leaning against the wind

Maastricht Treaty

Managed floating exchange–rate system

Optimum currency areas

Multiple Choice Questions

1. Which of the following is a benefit of a fixed exchange rate system?

a) Government chooses the exchange rate.

b) Nations can choose different inflation paths.

c) External imbalances produce changes in the money supply.

d) It is stabilizing in the presence of internally generated disturbances.

2. Which of the following is a benefit of a floating exchange rate system?

a) It frees monetary policy.

b) It is generally less efficient.

c) It imposes inflationary discipline.

d) It reduces the risk associated with international exchange.

3. Of the pairs below, which pair would most likely benefit most from a currency area?

a) New York and New Jersey.

b) Hawaii and Iceland.

c) Australia and France.

d) South Africa and Quebec.

4. A nation's currency board cannot

a) Hold foreign exchange reserves.

b) Buy its currency if it is depreciating.

c) Sell its currency if it is depreciating.

d) Increase the money supply to combat recession.

5. The Maastricht Treaty established
a) The Euro.
b) Dollarization.
c) The European Monetary System.
d) The criteria necessary for future members to adopt the euro.

6. In a managed float, the long-run exchange rate is determined by
a) The anchor.
b) Government.
c) A currency board.
d) Market forces.

7. Dollarization occurs when a nation
a) Adopts the dollar's inflation rate.
b) Adopts the dollar as its own currency.
c) Protects their currency by selling dollars.
d) Protects their currency by adding dollars to reserves.

8. Suppose a nation's exports fall due to recession abroad. If a nation has a freely floating exchange rate then which of the following will most likely happen? The nation's exchange rate will
a) Appreciate and offset some of the decreased demand for its goods.
b) Depreciate and offset some of the decreased demand for its goods.
c) Appreciate and amplify the decreased demand for its goods.
d) Depreciate and amplify the decreased demand for its goods.

9. Within an optimum currency area
a) Capital and labor are not mobile.
b) Exchange rates can float.
c) There is one central bank.
d) Unemployment will not occur.

10. Which of the following would not be advised for a nation that has experienced difficulty in controlling inflation?
a) Flexible exchange rates.
b) A currency board.
c) Dollarization.
d) Fixed exchange rates.

Problems and Discussion Questions

1. a) Why is a flexible exchange-rate system considered more efficient for the allocation of resources?

b) If a flexible exchange-rate system allocates resources better, then why have the EU countries adopted the euro?

2. a) What is the view of speculation that supports a fixed exchange rate system?

b) What is the view of speculation that supports a floating exchange rate system?

3. Suppose a nation is subject to many internal changes, e.g. volatile investment, domestic inflation, bumper crops, drought, etc. Explain whether the nation would be better off, other things being equal, with fixed rates or floating rates.

4. "The anchor argument assumes that it is easier to commit to an exchange rate than to an acceptable rate of inflation." Explain.

5. a) A nation chooses an inflation rate that is somewhat higher than most of its trading partners. What kind of exchange-rate system should the nation choose?

b) A nation's decides to lower it inflation rate to that of its largest trading partner. What kind of exchange-rate system would be useful in reducing inflation?

6. Why would it be difficult for the nations of Latin America to quickly adopt one currency?

7. Who bears the costs and uncertainties of a flexible exchange rate, and who bears the costs and uncertainties of a fixed exchange rate.

Chapter 16
The International Monetary System: Past, Present, and Future

Chapter Outline

Chapter Summary and Review

The purpose of an **international monetary system** is to promote the international exchange of goods, services and factors of production. A complete description of an international monetary system would include all of what is known as the **"rules of the game"**, which includes the conventions, organizations, and institutions by which nations agree to settle payments, adjust to payments imbalances and the nature of the exchange rate system. Exchange rate systems, as described in Chapter 15, can be fixed, freely floating, or anywhere in between. To the degree that governments intervene in foreign exchange markets, there is a need for a **reserve asset** for intervention purposes. If exchange rates are pegged to the dollar, then the dollar will tend to be the reserve asset. If a nation's currency moved below its fixed value, reserves would be used by the nation to buy its own currency. If a nation's currency moved above its fixed value, a nation would sell its currency for the dollar, adding to its reserves of dollars. If exchange rates are pegged to gold, then gold will tend to be the reserve asset.

Three important characteristics of an international monetary system are **adjustment, liquidity and confidence**. Adjustment describes the mechanisms that nations choose to adjust to external imbalances. Liquidity is the degree to which reserves are available to intervene in the foreign exchange market. If reserves are not in ample supply, then nations are forced to quickly contract the economy to reduce imports to eliminate deficits, or increase interest rates to attract financial flows. Liquidity is not necessary in a freely floating exchange rate system because governments do not intervene in such a system. Confidence describes the faith that nations have in the international monetary system, including the fairness of the adjustment mechanism, and the confidence in the value of reserves that are held to finance imbalances.

Fixed Exchange-Rate Systems

The gold standard, in operation from 1880-1914, was a fixed exchange-rate system in which each participating nation agreed to maintain some domestic price of gold, making gold the reserve asset. With each nation's currency fixed to gold, there is an implied fixed exchange rate with each other nation's currency. For example, if the price of gold in the US were to be set at $5 and the price of gold in the U.K. were to be set at £1, then the implied fixed price of the pound is $5/£1. If the United States were to run a deficit relative to the United Kingdom, then the price of the pound would begin to increase on the foreign exchange market, say to $5.10/£1. The discrepancy between the implied price of the pound due to established gold prices and the foreign exchange market price of gold would set off a movement of currencies and gold. For example, anyone with dollars would buy gold in the US at $5 and ship the gold to the U.K. and receive £1. The pound could then be sold on the foreign exchange market for $5.10, producing a profit of $0.10, before netting out the cost of shipping the gold. The buying of gold in the US would threaten to increase the price of gold, but the price of gold is to be set at $5. The monetary authorities in the US would have to sell gold for dollars, which reduces the money supply of the US The reduction in the US money supply would cause prices (and income) to fall in the United States, which would correct the US external deficit by stimulating exports and reducing imports.

This is the familiar price-specie-flow mechanism of Hume's, described in Chapter 13. In a gold standard, each nation, by agreeing to fix the price of gold, gives up control of its money supply in order to maintain a fixed exchange rate. By the rules of the game, nations with deficits do not offset (*sterilize*) the effects of gold movements on the money supply by changing the money supply through other means, although partial sterilization did occur in order to mitigate the domestic effects of the adjustment mechanism. A problem with this vision of the gold standard is the monetary reductions often worked to decrease domestic income as well as prices. Deficit countries often had to accept recession as part of the adjustment mechanism.

World War I disrupted the gold standard as economies experienced different conditions, which made the maintenance of fixed exchange rates impossible. The system was further strained by the Depression as nations experienced economic contraction to different degrees. To deal with unemployment, nations devalued their currencies (and implemented tariffs) in an attempt to switch demand to their products. This has the effect, however, of increasing unemployment in other nations, to which the other nations responded by implementing similar policies. These competitive devaluations and beggar-thy-neighbor policies set the stage for the next international monetary system, the **Bretton Woods system**.

The Bretton Woods system is named after the rural town in New Hampshire where delegates of 44 nations met to construct a new international monetary system that would be monitored by the International Monetary Fund (IMF), established just for that purpose. In the Bretton Woods system, the United States occupied center stage. The United States agreed to fix the price of gold at $35 per ounce, and the other member nations would fix their currency to the dollar, with ±1% deviations allowed, for a total bandwidth of 2%. Thus the Bretton Woods system is known as a "gold-exchange standard." To maintain the band, nations would use reserves of dollars to intervene in the foreign exchange market. The dollar was both the reserve asset and the **intervention currency**. Reserves can be held in any form if they can be readily exchanged for the intervention currency. At the time, however, only the dollar possessed full currency convertibility, so it was both the reserve asset and the intervention currency. Reserves of dollars could be earned when a nation's currency was strong. A strong currency meant its value threatened to appreciate relative to the dollar, requiring that the currency be sold for dollars. Reserves of dollars could also be borrowed from the IMF.

The IMF funded its lending to member nations through initial contributions made by member nations. The initial total contribution to the fund was $8.8 billion, with each nation contributing (subscribing) a percentage (quota) based on the economic importance of each country in world trade. Twenty-five percent of the contribution was made in gold, with the remainder made in its own currency. Member nations could borrow funds from the IMF, with borrowing above the initial contribution in gold subject to conditions and higher interest rates. The IMF policy of imposing conditions on the national economic policies of borrowing nations is known as **IMF conditionality**.

The lending facilities of the IMF contributed to the liquidity of the fixed exchange–rate system. In addition, the member nations of the IMF agreed to accept a new reserve asset called **Special Drawing Rights (SDRs)**. Special drawing rights were essentially accounting entries that member nations agreed to create and accept as reserve assets exchangeable for their own currencies. A nation could use its SDR allocation to buy dollars to intervene in the foreign exchange market and support their own currency. SDRs were not used for private transactions.

Exchange rates were to be changed only when absolutely necessary, which was known as **fundamental disequilibrium**, which was not defined precisely, but was understood to mean continual and sizeable deficits or surpluses. Exchange rate changes of less than 10% could be undertaken without IMF approval. In practice, devaluations were infrequent during the span of the Bretton Woods system, despite the apparent need for such devaluations. The consequence was persistent surpluses and deficits, which became apparent and so sparked destabilizing speculation, which only made the deficits and surpluses more pronounced.

Once the new international monetary system was underway, nations were expected to remove restrictions on currency exchange that were introduced after the breakdown of the gold standard, although restrictions on currency exchange for financial flows could remain to stem possible destabilizing speculation. In addition, trade barriers would be removed under the auspices of GATT.

The basic purpose of the IMF was to promote monetary stability by providing the liquidity necessary to maintain relatively fixed exchange rates. The IMF's sister organization, the **World Bank,** also known as the **International Bank for Reconstruction and Development (IBRD)** would finance long-term loans to help reconstruct the economies damaged by war and provide long-term development loans for the developing economies.

From 1945-1949 the US economy was the source of goods for the war-damaged economies of Europe, and the United States ran considerable surpluses. By 1950, and continuing until 1957, these surpluses became small deficits. These deficits were instrumental in that the net outflow of dollars supplied the liquidity necessary to European countries to maintain dollar reserve balances consistent with expanded trade and expanded external imbalances. Recall that the dollar was both the reserve and intervention currency. Dollar reserves were willingly held because they could be converted to gold at a fixed price, and dollar balances earned interest that gold did not.

From 1958 until the early 1970s, US deficits increased, reflecting large private direct investment in Europe and the high rate of inflation associated with the Vietnam War. Holdings of dollars by both foreign governments (reserve balances) and private sectors increased substantially. The United States could have devalued the dollar to correct the deficit but chose not to in order to maintain confidence in the dollar, which was viewed as necessary for the continued functioning of the dollar as a reserve asset. Devaluation of the dollar (a higher price for gold) would have reduced the value of foreign–held dollar reserves and possibly have led to a crisis of confidence. Instead, the United States instituted a number of policies, including direct controls, which would hopefully stem the outflow of dollars. By 1970, some foreign dollar balances had been converted to gold in the United States so US gold balances fell, while foreign holdings of dollars continued to increase. By 1970, outstanding dollars were four times as great as US gold holdings.

By 1971, it had become apparent that the dollar needed to be devalued, which led to huge destabilizing speculative dollar outflows. Unable to satisfy the speculative sales of dollars with gold, the United States suspended convertibility of the dollar into gold in mid–1971, marking the end of the Bretton Woods system. An attempt was made to maintain fixed exchange rates by devaluing the dollar and revaluing the German mark and the Japanese yen, the principal surplus countries relative to the United States.

At the new currency values, the band was widened from 1 percent to 2.25 percent, but the dollar was no longer convertible into gold, so this new system, called the **Smithsonian Agreement**, was a genuine **dollar standard**, in which no currency was pegged to gold.

Under the Bretton Woods dollar-exchange standard, exchange rates were allowed to change when there was a fundamental disequilibrium. In practice, exchange rates changed very little, despite the obvious need for devaluations and revaluations. Especially problematic was the need for a devaluation of the dollar, the center of the system. It was necessary for reserves to grow in order to provide *liquidity*, so the Bretton Woods system needed US deficits to continue to function well, but such deficits threatened the *confidence* of the world's reserve asset. National policy makers were reluctant to allow adjustment of the domestic economy because this meant recession in deficit countries and inflation in surplus countries. Without a smooth adjustment mechanism and problems with liquidity and confidence, the system ended.

Flexible Rates

The relatively fixed exchange–rate system of the Bretton Woods era has been replaced by increased flexibility of exchange rates. Many smaller countries peg to their major trading partners, and the EU has adopted one monetary system, but the remaining countries of the North and many large countries of the South have moved to a managed floating system, in which intervention is used to smooth short–term exchange rate fluctuations. Under the new floating system, reserves are still necessary for short-term interventions, and the IMF has expanded its lending facilities.

As might be expected, the problems associated with the current system of more flexible exchange rates, combined with freer movements of capital, include excessive volatility of exchange rates, and periodic financial crises, especially in emerging market economies.

Excessive short-run volatility can disrupt international trade and investment. In addition, there appears to be excessive long-run volatility. The United States, for example, experienced a period of continued appreciation in the early 1980s, followed by a period of continued depreciation in the late 1980s, and since the introduction of the euro in 1999, a general fall in the value of the dollar relative to the euro. Suggestions for reform of the system generally include more stability of exchange rates, which require some form of macroeconomic policy coordination. If nations have different inflation goals, then this is not possible and floating exchange rates are necessary. Professor James Tobin of Yale has suggested that floating rates move excessively because of very short-term capital flows (hot money) and has proposed a tax (now called the **Tobin Tax**) on such transactions that increases as the duration of the flow decreases.

In the past few years a number of emerging market economies (Mexico, south-East Asia, Russia and Brazil) have experienced financial crises, all due to substantial outflows of short-term funds in response to a lack of confidence. This lack of confidence is due to suspect banking and financial institutions.

Because of the difficulty of close macroeconomic policy coordination between countries, it appears that flexible exchange rates are here to stay for some time, with some intervention to reduce short-term fluctuations, and perhaps some attention to wide bands with limited policy coordination. In addition, financial crises in emerging market economies can be ameliorated by improved information flows (early-warning signals), improved safety of banking and financial institutions (more prudent monitoring and standards), and increased financial backing from both private and official (including IMF) at the first signs of crisis.

Key Terms used in Chapter Summary and Review
(The list below is not necessarily the same as the list provided by the Salvatore text.)

Adjustment	Intervention currency
Bretton Woods system	Liquidity
Confidence	Rules of the game
Dollar standard	Reserve asset
Fundamental disequilibrium	Smithsonian Agreement
IMF conditionality	Special Drawing Rights (SDRs)
International Bank for Reconstruction and	Tobin Tax
Development (IBRD)	World Bank
International monetary system	

Multiple Choice Questions

1. Which of the following best describes an international reserve asset?
a) Foreign exchange.
b) Assets held by banks.
c) Funds lent by the IBRD.
d) An asset held by countries to help stabilize exchange rates.

2. Liquidity refers to the
a) Degree of flexibility in exchange rates.
b) Transferability of funds held by the World Bank.
c) Adequacy of reserves
d) Ease of adjustment.

3. The Bretton Woods system was a
a) Gold standard.
b) Gold exchange standard.
c) Dollar standard.
d) Freely floating exchange rate system.

4. In the gold standard adjustment to external balances occurred through
a) Devaluation.
b) Revaluation.
c) Changes in the money supply.
d) Fiscal policy.

5. IMF conditionality refers to the conditions imposed by the IMF on
a) The size of loans.
b) National economic policies.
c) The allocation of SDR's
d) The rules of the game.

6. In the gold-exchange standard, the dollar was pegged to gold and
a) Other currencies were pegged to gold.
b) Other currencies were pegged to the dollar.
c) Other currencies exchanged freely.
d) Gold was the reserve asset.

7. The SDR
a) Is a reserve asset.
b) Was created by the US.
c) Was created by the World Bank.
d) Is necessary with floating rates.

8. Flexible exchange rates are necessary when
a) Liquidity is very high.
b) Adjustment is considered fair.
c) Nations do not coordinate policies.
d) Nations pursue very similar inflation policies.

9. If there were fundamental disequilibrium for a currency under the Bretton Woods system then

a) The currency's value could not be changed.

b) The currency became a freely floating currency.

c) Speculation would most likely be destabilizing.

d) A Tobin Tax would be imposed.

10. Relative to the Bretton Woods system, the current international monetary system is marked by

a) A greater role for the dollar as a reserve asset.

b) Greater flexibility of exchange rates.

c) Greater policy coordination.

d) An expanded role for gold.

Problems and Discussion Questions

1. a) What are the "rules of the game" in the gold standard?

b) What are the "rules of the game" in the Bretton Woods system?

2. a) What was the dilemma associated with the relationship between liquidity and confidence in the Bretton Woods system?

b) Explain how the creation and distribution of SDRs was an attempt to settle the dilemma explained in part a).

3. a) What automatic adjustments to an external deficit would occur under the Bretton Woods system?

b) How could policy makers resist the automatic adjustment mechanism? Why would policy makers resist the automatic adjustment mechanism?

c) What problems would resistance to the automatic adjustment mechanism create?

4. a) What was the historical context in which the Bretton Woods system of relatively fixed exchange rates was created?

b) What was the role of the IMF in the Bretton Woods system?

5. Why was destabilizing speculation a major problem in the Bretton Woods system?

6. a) Provide a brief description of the exchange-rate arrangements of the current international monetary system.

b) What are some of the major problems associated with the current international monetary system?

Solutions

Chapter 1: Introduction to the Global Economy

Multiple Choice Questions

1. b
2. d
3. c
4. d
5. c

Problems and Discussion Questions

1. a) In the case of increased imports of consumer goods, consumers will gain. In the case of increased imports of inputs (raw materials, physical capital, etc.), firms that produce with the inputs will gain.

b) Firms that produce products that compete with imports – import competing firms.

2. a) If each individual had to produce her own autos, clothes, coffee, etc. the individual's standard of living would undoubtedly be reduced.

b) It would be compromised because nations would be limited to those goods produce domestically. The nation could not take advantage of goods produced more cheaply abroad nor have access to the rich assortment of goods available abroad.

3. a) Autos, wine, cheese, computers, software, etc.

b) Land and personal services like haircuts.

c) Goods that are not traded tend to have very high transportation costs. In order for trade to occur, price differences between nations must exceed the transportation costs.

4. A major challenge is to address the concerns of the anti-globalization movement, which include, among other things, the environment and the ability to provide the gains from globalization to all individuals and nations.

Chapter 2: Comparative Advantage

Multiple Choice Questions

1. d
2. c
3. a
4. d
5. d
6. d
7. b
8. c
9. a
10. d

Problems and Discussion Questions

1. a) Cambodia has the absolute advantage in both goods.

b) Cambodia has the comparative advantage in Candles and Thailand has the comparative advantage in Incense.

c)

Changes in Production from Reallocating Two Units of Labor

	Thailand	Cambodia	World
Change in Candles	-2	+4	+2
Change in Incense	+6	-4	+2

d) Thailand has a comparative advantage in Incense, so Thailand will export Incense for Candles if the terms are favorable. Domestically Thailand can get 1 Candle for 3 units of Incense, so they will not trade if 3 units of Incense trade for 1 or less units of Candles.

e) Cambodia has a comparative advantage in Candles, so Cambodia will export Candles for Incense if the terms are favorable. Domestically Cambodia can get 4 units of Incense for 4 units of Candles so they will not trade if 4 units of Candles trade for less than 4 units of Incense.

f) Yes. For Thailand, 6 Incense for 4 Candles is better than 3 Incense for 1 Candle. For Cambodia, 4 Candles for 6 Incense is better than 4 Candles for 4 Incense.

g) In Thailand, $\Delta C/\Delta I = 1/3$, so Thailand will be willing to export Incense if the terms are greater than this, e.g., $\Delta C/\Delta I = 2/3$.
   In Cambodia $\Delta C/\Delta I = 4/4$, so Cambodia will be willing to export Candles if the terms are less than this, e.g., $\Delta C/\Delta I = 4/5$.

Thus, Thailand and Cambodia will both willingly trade if the terms of trade lie in between the nations' opportunity costs.

2. First note that the numbers represent the labor-hours per unit of output. (Question 1 used units of output per laborer.)

a) Upland has the absolute advantage in Good A because it can produce one unit with fewer hours. Overland has the absolute advantage in Good E.

b) In this particular case the comparative advantage for each nation is the same as the absolute advantage.

3. a) Each unit of Tin costs 2 units of Steel in Russia.

b) Each unit of Tin costs ½ unit of Steel in China.

c)

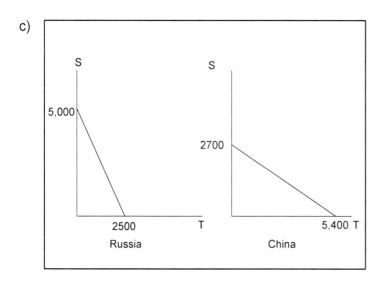

d) The slope of Russia's ppf is $\Delta S/\Delta T = 2$.
The slope of China's ppf is $\Delta S/\Delta T = ½$.

e) The slope of a ppf is equal to the opportunity cost of the good on the horizontal axis.

f) A linear ppf indicates a constant opportunity cost at all levels of production.

g) China.

h) Any terms of trade between the opportunity costs of Russian and China, so any $\Delta S/\Delta T$ between 2 and ½.

Solutions

i)

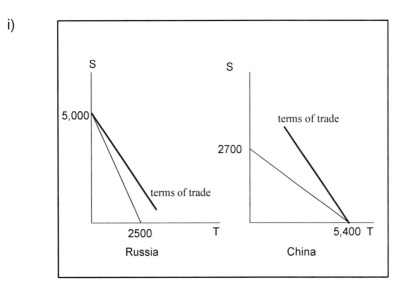

Russia

China

j) Each nation can trade along the terms of trade to a point outside its own ppf. Thus, with trade each nation can consume beyond its ability to produce in the absence of trade.

4. a)

Price of Steel and China

	Russia	China
Price of Steel	$1	$2
Price of Tin	$2	$1

b) No, China has the lower wage, but Russia has a lower price for Steel.

c) The productivity of labor.

d) No, because China would have lower prices in both goods at these wages. Trade would produce a higher demand for Chinese products and Chinese labor, causing an increase in Chinese wages.

5. The idea is illustrated for one nation in the diagram to the right. There is less than complete specialization at point G and complete specialization at point H. The terms of trade line from point H lies outside that from point G.

6. The tools (capital) and talent (education and training) possessed by that labor.

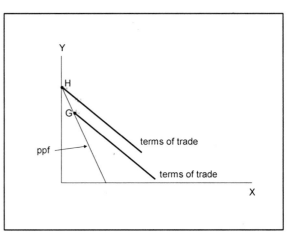

Chapter 3: The Standard Trade Model

Multiple Choice Questions

1. b
2. b
3. a
4. c
5. d
6. a
7. a
8. d
9. b
10. a

Problems and Discussion Questions

1. a)
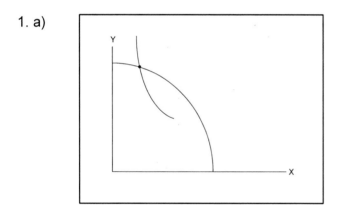

b) $MRS_{Y/X}$ exceeds the opportunity cost of X.

c) More X.

d) They are equal. Any inequality means a reallocation will improve welfare.

2. a) Any P_C/P_N above ½.

b) Any P_C/P_N below 4.

c) Any P_C/P_N between ½ and 4.

Solutions

d)

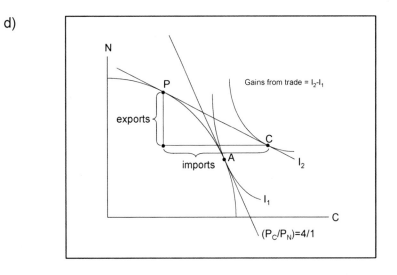

3. Complete specialization is less likely with increasing costs. With constant cost, a nation's comparative advantage is maintained no matter what the level of production so as production of the good with the comparative advantage increases the advantage still exists. Gains continue as production increases until production is completely specialized.

With increasing costs, specialization in a product increases the cost of production. As production of the good with the comparative advantage increases, the advantage will be lost. If the advantage is lost before complete specialization then specialization will be incomplete.

4. a)

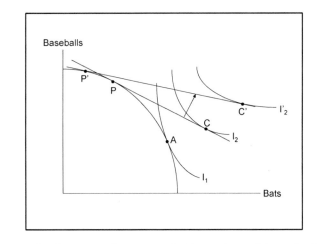

b) In the graph above an increase in the price of baseballs flattens the line along which trade can occur. The higher price of baseballs for a nation producing baseballs increases production from P to P', changes production from C to C', and makes the nation better off by the move from indifference curve I_2 to I'_2.

5. a) Yes, if they have different ppfs

b) Yes, if they have different preference maps.

c) No, the autarky prices would be identical.

Chapter 4: The Heckscher-Ohlin and Other Trade Theories

Multiple Choice Questions

1. d
2. a
3. c
4. a
5. a
6. b
7. c
8. a
9. c
10. d

Problems and Discussion Questions

1. a) Nation 2. The slope of the ppfs is the opportunity cost of computers. Because Nation 2's ppf is flatter at each production level of computers, Nation 2 has a comparative advantage in computers, so Nation 2 must be capital rich.

b) Not necessarily. Based on comparative advantage the most we can say is $(K/L)_2 > (K/L)_1$.

2. a) The diagram is drawn with Textiles as Nation 1's export good.

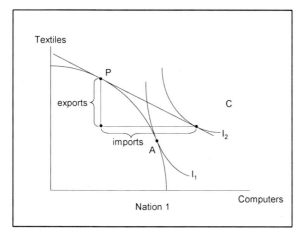

3. Before trade the nation is producing on its ppf at point A, and after trade the nation is producing at point P. Both points are on the ppf so there is full employment before and after trade.

4. a) Nation 2 is capital rich so labor is relatively expensive. Nation 2 has the higher w/r.

b) Nation 2's abundant factor is capital, so w/r will fall in Nation 2.

c) Laborers will lose in capital-rich Nation 2.

d) Owners of capital in capital-rich Nation 2 will gain.

5. a) If the only relevant aspect of intra-industry trade were product differentiation, then what is not explained is why nations simply do not produce all of the product variety demanded by its citizens.

b) If there are economies of scale, then a nation cannot produce a small amount of all varieties of products at a low cost because the production of each product would be relatively small. It is efficient for each nation to produce a large quantity of one or a few varieties of products in order to exploit economies of scale, and then trade the products to other nations specializing in other differentiated products.

6. Trade can occur if no nation has a comparative advantage in autarchy if there are economies of scale.

7. a) Japan is most likely capital-rich relative to Mexico, so Japanese workers will resist trade with Mexico. In Mexico, owners of capital will resist trade with Japan.

b) Yes, because there are gains from trade.

8. Children's toys. The other products have no or little differentiation. If there are economies of scale and little product differentiation, then one nation can produce at very low cost for other nations, but there will be no intra-industry trade. With the many varieties of children's toys, not one nation will be able to produce all varieties for itself and enjoy economies of scale.

Chapter 5: Trade Restrictions: Tariffs

Multiple Choice Questions

1. a
2. a
3. c
4. c
5. b
6. a
7. b

8. c
9. c
10. b

Problems and Discussion Questions

1. a) Demand by domestics.

b) $2

c) A small nation, because the $10 price is not changed when the $2 tariff is imposed. Before the tariff the imported good arrived at the border with a price of $10. After the $2 tariff the price is $12, so the good still arrives at the border with a price of $10.

d) It increases by $2.

2. a) Consumption effect is a reduction of 10 units.

b) Production effect is an increase of 20 units.

c) The trade effect is a reduction in imports of 30 units.

d) The revenue effect is $2x30 = $60.

3. a) $2x130 + ½($2x10) = $270.

b) $2x80 + ½($2x20) = $180.

c) $2x30 = $60

d) Net losses are $270-$180-$60 = -$30, which is the sum of b+d.

e) $30.

4. It's best to draw the supply and demand curves and then label the points given.

a) Consumer surplus lost = $224.

b) The two triangles the make the deadweight loss add to $28.

c) Zero. The optimum tariff argument only holds for a large country. This is a small country because the world price is unaffected by the tariff.

5. The domestic value added before the tariff is $400. The domestic value after the tariff increases the price to $1200, is $600. The effective rate of protection is the percent increase in domestic value added of 1/3, or 33.3%

6. Domestic value decreases from $400 to $280, so the effective rate of protection is the decrease in domestic value added of -$120/$400 = -30%.

Chapter 6: Nontariff Trade Barriers and the Political Economy of Protectionism

Multiple Choice Questions

1. a
2. b
3. a
4. c
5. a
6. b
7. d
8. a
9. a
10. b

Problems and Discussion Questions

1. a) $1.50.

b) $6,000.

c) The welfare loss of the quota when revenues are collected through the auction of import licenses will be identical to that of a tariff. The deadweight loss equals the sum of the two usual triangles, which is $3,000.

d) The welfare loss now includes not only the deadweight loss, but also the lost license revenue. The deadweight loss is $3,000, and the revenue lost is $6,000, so the total welfare loss is $9,000.

e) Because the VER is agreed to by the foreign nation, and the foreign nation receives some benefit ($9000 in this case), there will not be retaliation as with a unilaterally imposed quota.

f) $1.50.

2. a) It may not represent intent to harm US producers, but just a response to different price elasticities of demand.

b) No. If this dumping is due to a lower price elasticity of demand in the US, then it is permanent. The lower price in the US will be available permanently.

3. No, it may be simple comparative advantage.

4. The auto industry is highly organized, so it may be able to use the strength of its organization to exert pressure on elected representatives. In addition the auto industry is relatively geographically concentrated so that workers interests can more easily be represented at the voting booth.

The textile industry, like the auto industry is geographically concentrated. In addition, foreign textile exporters are located in nations with little economic and political power. They cannot easily resist trade protection from more powerful importing nations.

5. The increase in nontariff barriers is due to the success of GATT in lowering tariff barriers.

Chapter 7: Economic Integration

Multiple Choice Questions

1. c
2. a
3. b
4. d
5. c
6. c
7. a
8. b
9. a
10. d

Problems and Discussion Questions

1. Neighboring countries like Canada, Mexico and the US are often natural trading partners due to the low transportation costs. With low transportation costs, very small differences in comparative advantage can be exploited. If the bulk of trade is with neighboring nations, then a regional trading agreement with neighboring nations is likely to be trade creating.

Additionally, neighboring countries often share a history and culture that eases the negotiations process. Familiarity can also enhance trade because each nation is familiar with the demand patterns of other countries, making it easier to produce products for those countries.

2. a) If there are economies of scale then trade will allow each nation to specialize in one or a few products, letting other nations specialize in other products. The economies of scale will bring lower prices to all nations.

b) The gains from increased competition are gains from reductions in monopoly power.

c) The greater level of economic activity due to a customs union invites investment.

3. If a customs union is large enough, it will become a significant importer from the rest-of-the-world. Large importing countries can gain from imposing a tariff (optimum tariff argument), but world welfare will fall.

4. a) Prior to the formation of the customs union, a tariff is applied to all imports. Because S_m+T is lower than S_n+T, imports will come from future members. At a price of S_m+T, domestic production will be Q_3, domestic consumption will be Q_6, and imports will equal the difference between Q_6 and Q_3.

b) After formation of the customs union, members' price will fall to S_m, and the price from non-members will remain at S_n+T. Imports will continue to be from members at the new lower price. Domestic production will be Q_1, domestic consumption will be Q_8, and imports will equal the difference between Q_8 and Q_1.

c) The customs union will be trade creating because it will not cause a substitute of the source of imports. Imports will come from future members before formation of the customs union and from members after formation of the customs union.

d) Yes, there will necessarily be gains from the formation of the customs union, because no trade is diverted from non-members as a result of the formation of the customs union. The gains are the triangles equal to the deadweight losses associated with a tariff.

5. a)-d) In this case the future non-members' price plus tariff is lower than future member's price plus tariff, so all imports will come from non-members. After the customs union is formed, the non-members' price with the tariff is still below the members' price without the tariff. The customs unions will have no effect on the price at which imports will occur. The customs union will have no effect on domestic production, consumption, or imports. Domestic production before and after the customs union is Q_2, domestic consumption is Q_7, and imports are the difference between Q_7 and Q_2. The formation of the customs union produces no welfare changes because it has no effect on price. In such cases there is no incentive to form a customs union.

6. a) Prior to formation of the customs union the lowest price (plus tariff) is S_n+T, at which domestic production is Q_3, domestic consumption is Q_6, and imports equal Q_6-Q_3. All imports come from future non-members.

b) After formation of the customs union, the lowest price available is S_m, at which domestic production is Q_2, domestic consumption is Q_7, and imports are Q_7-Q_2. All imports come from members.

c) The customs union in this case is trade diverting because the formation of the customs union reduces trade from non-members, although it increases trade from members.

d) There will not necessarily be gains from the formation of this customs union. There will be the usual efficiency gains from a lower price equal to the triangles below S and D. (One triangle has a base of Q_3-Q_2 and a height of S_n+T-S_m. The other triangle has a base of Q_7-Q_6 and a height of S_n+T-S_m. Locate these on the diagram in Figure 7.3.) However, in addition to the usual efficiency gains from the lower price, there will be a loss equal to part of the former tariff revenues. This loss is equal to the rectangle with length Q_7-Q_3 and width S_n+T-S_m. (Locate this rectangle in Figure 7.3, and review the analysis by which this is identified as a loss that may offset the efficiency gains.)

Chapter 8: Growth and Development with International Trade

Multiple Choice Questions

1. d
2. c
3. c
4. c
5. d
6. b
7. a
8. b
9. d
10. c

Problems and Discussion Questions

1. a) Graph (ii).

b) Graph (iv).

c) Graph (i).

d) Graph (iii).

e) Graph (i).

2. a) If the stock of capital increases with no change in the labor force, then each labor will be able to produce more. Both total and per laborer income will increase, so per capita income will increase.

b) With an increased labor force but no change in capital, the amount produced by the new laborers will be less than the previous laborers, so although production increases, the amount produced per laborer will fall. With a constant dependency ratio, per capita income will fall.

c) If there are constant returns to scale, then total income increases and per capita income is unchanged.

d) Total income increases, and with no change in the labor force, per worker and per capita income will increase.

e) Same as d).

3. a) The commodity terms of trade is $N = (P_X/P_M)100$, so for 1992 the commodity terms of trade is $N_{1992} = (108.7/102.1)100 = 106.46$. Making the same substitutions for 1993 and 1994 produces:

$$N_{1993} = (104.5/99.9)100 = 104.60, \text{ and}$$
$$N_{1994} = (107.4/105.3)100 = 101.99.$$

b) There was deterioration in the commodity terms of trade for Mauritius from 1992–94. The price of exports relative to the price paid for imports fell, suggesting that Mauritius received less imports for each *unit* of exports.

c) The income terms of trade are expressed as $I = (P_X/P_M) Q_X$. Substituting from the table in Question 3 produces

$$I_{1992} = (108.7/102.1)100 = 106.46$$
$$I_{1993} = (104.5/99.9)104.2 = 109.00, \text{ and}$$
$$I_{1994} (104.5/99.9)105.1 = 109.94.$$

If the 1992 income terms of trade is set to 100, and the 1993 and 1994 adjusted accordingly (dividing by 106.46 and multiplying the result by 100), then the income terms of trade index for those years will be

$$I_{1992} = 100$$
$$I_{1993} = 102.39$$
$$I_{1994} = 103.27.$$

d) Although the commodity terms of trade fell from 1992–94, the income terms of trade improved. The reduction in export prices relative to import prices was more than compensated for by an increase in the quantity exported.

4. a) The long-run experience has been negative. Although ISI may be useful in promoting employment and industrialization in the short run, the use of the policy in the long run creates the demand for additional imported inputs to support the industrial base. Additionally, the need for skilled labor becomes a constraint after the initial easy phases of ISI have been completed.

b) ISI attempts to replace imported goods with domestic production. If the goods were initially imported, then other nations have the comparative advantage in these goods. Export-oriented growth relies on a nation's comparative advantage, and so makes better use of a nation's resources. Export-oriented growth is less likely to get bogged down by the necessity for imported inputs, and the necessary labor is available in the domestic market.

5. It depends upon the cause of the shift of the ppf. If the shift is due to more labor with no change in other factors of production or technology, then diminishing returns will occur and production per laborer will decrease. If the shift is due to more capital with no change in other factors of production or technology, then the productivity per laborer will increase, so production per capita will increase.

6. a) Primary goods have both lower supply and demand price elasticities than other goods. When supply shifts, or when demand shifts, the excess supply or demand requires a larger price change to produce a new equilibrium. Visually, when the supply and demand curves are steep, a shift in either one will cause a larger price change than when the curves are flat.

b) A buffer stock absorbs excess supply and demand so that the price does not change on the market. The export good should be added to its buffer stock when there is excess supply of the good. This will keep the price of the good from falling on world markets. When there is excess demand the good should be sold from the buffer stock in order to keep its price from increasing on world markets. This promotes stable prices through time, which can make planning easier at both the production level and at the national policy level.

Chapter 9: International Resource Movements and Multinational Corporations

Multiple Choice Questions

1. a
2. c
3. d
4. b

5. c
6. a
7. d
8. c
9. b
10. d

Problems and Discussion Questions

1. a) The United States is capital rich relative to Mexico, so the US will export capital-intensive goods to Mexico. If, however, capital is mobile internationally, then capital may also move to Mexico. Both trade in products and movement of factors can represent the different endowments of countries.

b) Mexico is labor rich relative to the United States so Mexico' wages will be lower relative to US wages, producing a movement of labor from Mexico to the US.

c) The movement of capital from the US to Mexico will raise the returns to capital in the US and lower the return to capital in Mexico until returns are equalized. The movement of labor from Mexico to the US will raise wages in Mexico and lower wages in the US until wages are equalized.

d) According to the factor-price equalization theorem, trade in goods will equalize both absolute and relative factor prices. Thus, trade will increase the wage rate in Mexico and decrease it in the United States until wages are equalized. Similarly, the return to capital will decrease in Mexico and increase in the United States until the returns are equalized. Trade produces the same changes factor prices as the movement of the factors.

2. a) In competitive markets, real wages will reflect the (marginal) productivity of labor. If real wages are not equal, then productivities are not equal. If labor moves from low to high wage areas, then they are moving to where productivity is higher. The movement to higher productivity areas means an increase in world production. The same argument applies for the movement of capital from low return areas to high return areas.

b) Labor in the United States will lose as the wage rate is driven down by the increased supply of labor. This may create greater income inequality because the type of labor most likely to lose in the US is unskilled labor with low wages. In Mexico the wages of unskilled workers will increase, so income inequality is likely to decrease.

3. a) There is the fear by the home country that MNCs will provide jobs abroad that would otherwise have gone to local citizens. There is also the fear that technological know-how will be transferred abroad, resulting in a loss of any technically based competitive edge.

b) The basic fear on the part of host countries is dependency. MNCs have no allegiance to the host country so their economic, political, and social influence in the host country may not necessarily be in the host country's interest.

4. MNCs have a number of advantages over firms in local markets. One is sheer size. Sheer size brings political clout, maybe monopoly power, economies of scale, and the ability to locate stages of production in those nations where the cost of production is lower. The vast information network of MNCs also allows for superior methods of distribution, advertising, and control. The ability to engage in transfer pricing may also allow MNCs to pay lower tax rates than local firms.

5. a) No. If the only motivation for foreign portfolio investment is return, then funds will simply flow towards the nation with the higher return. There will be a one-way movement of capital.

b) Diversification allows financial investors to reduce risk without affecting the rate of return. Diversification requires funds to be spread over many markets. As new wealth is created each year, the diversification of new funds will flow to all countries simultaneously.

6. To the extent that trade in products is a substitute for the movement of factors, freer trade with Mexico will reduce Mexican migration to the US and the movement of US capital to Mexico. If Mexico cannot realize gains from selling their labor-intensive products to the US, then that unskilled labor has an incentive to move to the US to realize their advantage. Similarly if the US cannot export their capital-intensive products to Mexico, then cheap capital will flow from the US to Mexico.

Chapter 10: Balance of Payments

Multiple Choice Questions

1. a
2. d
3. a
4. c
5. d
6. a
7. d
8. b
9. a
10. c

Problems and Discussion Questions

1. a) If the US exports (credit) are to be paid for in three months, then the US firm is extending a short-term loan to France — a short-term capital outflow (debit). The entry is:

	Credit (+)	Debit (-)
Exports	$500	
ST Capital (outflow)		$500

b) The imports (debit) by the US from the U. K. are paid for by buying pounds from a U.K. bank. The U.K. bank willingly acquires dollars, a claim on US goods, so the bank is lending to the United States — a short-term capital inflow (credit). The entry is:

	Credit (+)	Debit (-)
Imports		$400
ST Capital (inflow)	$400	

c) If you spent $300 in the United Kingdom, then someone in the United Kingdom has accepted US dollars. As in b) this is short-term capital inflow. The actual expenditures are recorded as "tourist services" provided (debit) and the holding of funds by someone in the United Kingdom is recorded as a short-term capital inflow.

	Credit (+)	Debit (-)
Tourist Services		$300
ST Capital (inflow)	$300	

d) This is unilateral transfer provided to another nation (debit), and the other nation willingly holds the dollars, a short-term capital inflow (credit).

	Credit (+)	Debit (-)
Unilateral Transfer		$200
ST Capital (outflow)	$200	

e) The stock transfer is a long-term capital outflow (debit). The sale of Belgian Euros by a US bank represents a reduction in foreign assets held, a short-term capital inflow (credit).

	Credit (+)	Debit (-)
LT Capital (outflow)		$100
ST Capital (inflow)	$100	

f) The purchase of short-term assets in the United States by a foreigner is short-term capital inflow (credit). The purchase of dollars from a US bank means the US bank acquires pounds, a foreign asset — a short-term capital outflow (debit).

	Credit (+)	Debit (-)
ST Capital (inflow)	$50	
ST Capital (outflow)		$50

2. a)

US Balance of Payments

Account	Credit (+)	Debit (-)
Merchandise Exports	$500	
Merchandise Imports		$400
Tourist Services		$300
Unilateral Transfers		$200
Long-Term Capital		$100
Short-Term Capital	$500	
Balance	**$1000**	**$1000**

b) The balance of trade is in surplus by $100 (Merchandise Exports minus Merchandise Imports).

c) The balance of trade in goods and services in this example includes Merchandise Exports, Merchandise Imports, and Tourist Services. These net out to a deficit of $200.

d) The current account in this example includes the balance of trade in goods and services (part c), plus Unilateral Transfers. These balances net out to a deficit of $400.

e) The capital account includes both short-term and long-term capital movements, which nets out to a surplus of $400.

f) The entire balance of payments balances. The capital account is in surplus by the exact amount that the current account is in deficit. This will always be the case because total credits and debits must equal.

3. a) It is meaningless to speak of a balance of payments deficit or surplus if *all* account balances are included in the balance of payments. When all accounts are included, the net balance must always net to zero.

b) It is meaningful to speak of a balance of payments deficit or surplus if the balance of payments is defined to include all *autonomous* flows. In a fixed exchange rate system autonomous flows need not net to zero. The balance for all autonomous flows is that which must be financed by official capital flows. Note that the total value of autonomous and official flows will still net to zero. (In a fixed exchange–rate system, the exchange rate moves to equalize all autonomous inflows and outflows, so the autonomous flows will always net to zero.)

4. The capital account in Questions 1 and 2 is in surplus by $400. This means that foreigners have acquired *new* claims on the United States by, net, $400. Thus the United States has increased its foreign indebtedness by, net, $400. This increased debt represents the financing of the current account deficit.

5. a) The international investment position of the United States, measured in either historical, replacement, or market terms, turned from positive to negative beginning around 1985. This means the United States went from being a net creditor nation to a net debtor nation relative to the rest of the world. This change in the international investment position of the United States reflects the large current account deficits of the 1980s, requiring capital inflows.

b) The benefit of such inflows is that the US can support consumption and investment levels higher than it could have without such capital inflow.

c) Capital inflows occur in anticipation of a rate of return. If the capital inflows financed productive investment with substantial returns, then the returns that will be paid to foreigners can be easily paid. If, however the capital inflows financed consumption, then it could represent a considerable future burden (much like borrowing for a vacation now, only to find the repayment a drain on day-to-day living in the future.) In addition, an abrupt withdrawal of funds by foreigners could produce a financial crisis, with pressures on both the exchange rate and the interest rate.

Chapter 11: The Foreign Exchange Market and Exchange Rates

Multiple Choice Questions

1. c
2. a
3. b
4. c
5. d
6. b
7. d
8. a
9. c
10. c

Problems and Discussion Questions

1. Your diagrams should have quantity of yen on the horizontal axis and dollars per yen on the vertical axis.

a) The demand for yen will shift to the right (increase) as those with dollars buy interest bearing assets in Japan. In addition, the supply of yen will shift to the left (decrease) as those with yen seek fewer dollars as they shift from US interest-bearing assets to Japanese interest-bearing assets. Both shifts will produce an increase in the dollar price of the yen.

b) A decrease in US income lowers US imports so fewer yen are demanded (demand curve shifts left), causing the dollar price of the yen to fall.

c) Japan will import more from the US so the Japanese will supply more yen (supply of yen shifts to the right) to buy dollars in order to import, producing a decrease in the dollar price of the yen.

d) US inflation will lead both the US and Japan to switch purchases to Japan. This will produce an increased demand for the yen (demand for yen shifts to the right) and a reduced supply of the yen (supply of yen shifts to the left), both of which will cause an increase in the dollar price of the yen.

2. a) Uncovered interest parity is expressed as
$$i = i^* + [E(SR)-SR]/SR.$$
Covered interest parity is expressed as
$$i = i^* + [FR-SR]/SR.$$
The two are equivalent except that FR replaces E(SR). If both conditions hold, then
$$FR= E(SR).$$
This says that the current forward rate equals what the spot rate is expected to be in the future (both being expressed for the same time horizon).

b) The direct cause is simply that a difference will lead to speculation that will eliminate the difference. For example, suppose that FR > E(SR). Speculators will sell now in the forward market, expecting to buy the currency to satisfy the forward contract at a lower price in the future. Selling at the high FR will cause it to fall. This will continue until there is no possibility of profit, which occurs when FR = E(SR).

c) The equality between FR and E(SR) is unlikely to hold because it is risky. Speculators may not be willing to sell at FR, expecting to buy at a lower SR in the future, unless the difference is large enough to compensate for the risk undertaken. FR and E(SR) will differ by a risk premium called the "exchange-risk premium."

3 a) Assuming that IBM wants to realize its profits/losses in dollars, IBM risks a depreciation of the yen. If the dollar value of the yen falls (depreciation), then when the yen receipts are converted to dollars, they will yield a lower amount of dollars than at contract time.

b) IBM can sell the expected yen proceeds in the forward market on a continual basis. If it is expected that one million yen will be received in each month for some number of months in the future, then IBM can sell yen in the forward market each month. IBM still will be exposed to risk, however, for the forward rate can change from month to month. To eliminate that risk, IBM would have to sell yen on the forward market for next month, the following month, etc. all in the current period.

c) IBM can agree to swap yen in the future for dollars at a rate determined today. Currency swaps can be arranged over any time period, so the swap could be arranged for each of the next twelve months, or longer. The swap involves only one contract whereby doing the same thing in the forward contract would require a number of contracts.

4. a) The pound has two different prices. Arbitragers will exploit the difference, buying pounds in Bonn and selling them in Tokyo, profiting by five cents per pound. Buying in the cheap market will force the price up and selling in the high-price market will force the price down, until the prices are equalized in the two markets.

b) Pounds can be acquired directly in New York for $1.45 per pound. Alternatively, Euros can be bought in London for $.20 per Euro and then used to buy pounds in Paris. If $1.40 is used to buy Euros in London, then 7 Euros can be bought. The 7 Euros can then buy one pound in Paris. It is five cents cheaper to go through London and Paris to get pounds than buying them directly in New York.

c) It is a disequilibrium situation because it will set off buying and selling until the prices change. Arbitragers will buy Euros in London and use them to buy pounds in Paris. For example, with $100, 500 Euros can be purchased in London. The 500 Euros will buy 71.43 pounds in Paris, which when sold in New York will yield $13.57, a gain of $3.57 over the original $100. A Euro will cost $0.20 dollars in London and buy 7 pounds i for $1.40 per pound and sell them in New York for $1.45 per pound. The buying in London and Paris will drive up prices there, and the selling in New York will drive the prices down there, until the cost of acquiring a pound is the same everywhere.

5. If it is expected that the dollar cost of a yen will increase, then you could simply convert dollars to yen now and wait for the price increase. This method requires a consideration of the difference in interest rates. Getting out of the dollar now means foregoing the interest rate paid on dollars and receiving the interest rate paid on yen deposits.

Alternatively, yen could be bought in the forward market. If the price of yen does increase, then they can be bought at the previously contracted low forward price and sold at the new higher price. The advantage in using the forward market is, except for a small good-faith deposit, no funds need to be used.

Finally, an option to buy yen could be purchased. If the yen does increase in value, then the option can be exercised, buying yen at the low option price, and selling it at the new higher price. The advantage of using the option market is that the option need not be exercised unless it is to the speculator's advantage. An option contract need not be exercised while a forward contract must be honored. The disadvantage is the option has a price of its own, while a forward contract has no cost.

6. a) The U.K. firm should buy Euros in the forward market now.

b) The U.S. bank should sell Euros in the forward market now.

c) The security will deliver dollars in one year, so the Canadian investor should sell dollars in the forward market now. (Although regular forward markets do not exist for one year, they can be negotiated through commercial banks.)

d) Japanese yen are owed so the U.S. firm should buy Japanese yen in the forward market now.

e) No forward transaction is necessary. When the yen debt comes due, the U.S. importer will be receiving yen, which can be used to pay the debt. The U.S. importer has already received the dollars by borrowing yen and converting to dollars. The point of the question is to show how borrowing can be used in the same way as the forward market.

7. The domestic (assumed to be the U.S.) interest rate exceeds the return from investing in a foreign asset, including the gain or loss from covering in the forward market. Funds will flow to the U.S. so the dollar cost of foreign currency, SR, will fall. As SR falls, [FR-SR]/SR will increase. There will also be less forward sales (reduced supply) of the forward currency so FR will increase, also causing [FR-SR]/SR to increase. This will continue until

$$i = i^* + [FR-SR]/SR.$$

In addition to the effects on the spot and forward rates, the movement of funds to the United States will cause i to fall and i^* to increase, which also moves the inequality towards equality. Summarizing, if $i > i^* + [FR-SR]/SR$, then the movement of funds will cause interest rates and currency rates to change until there is equality of i and $i^* + [FR-SR]/SR$.

Chapter 12: Exchange Rate Determination

Multiple Choice Questions

1. c
2. c
3. a
4. b

Solutions

5. b
6. d
7. b
8. a
9. c
10. c

Problems and Discussion Questions

1. a) The demand for the Euro will increase (demand shifts right) and the supply of the Euro will decrease (supply of Euro shifts left) so the Euro will appreciate.

b) Europe will import more from the US, increasing the supply of Euros (supply shifts right), which will cause a depreciation of the Euro.

c) If the dollar is expected to appreciate, then the supply of Euros will increase (supply shifts right) as those with Euros seek the dollar, which is expected to become more valuable. In addition, the demand for Euros will decrease (demand shifts left) as those with dollars will want to buy fewer Euros. Both effects will cause the Euro to depreciate.

2. a) The demand for the dollar will decrease and the supply of the dollar will increase, both of which will lead to a depreciation of the dollar.

b) Europe will import more from the US so the demand for the dollar will increase, which causes an appreciation of the dollar.

c) The demand for the dollar will increase and the supply of the dollar will decrease, both of which will lead to an appreciation of the dollar.

3. a) The real exchange rate is defined as $(P^{¥})(R)/P^{\$}$, and absolute PPP exists when $R = P^{\$}/P^{¥}$. Substituting for R in the real exchange rate produces a value of 1.0. If absolute PPP holds, then the real exchange rate is equal to 1.0.

b) If absolute PPP holds, then the exchange rate reflects the relative price levels, so converting $10 into candy bars in the United States would yield the same number of candy bars as converting $10 into yen and then into candy bars in Japan.

4. a) Yes. If the law of one price holds for all traded goods, then a dollar will buy the same amount of traded goods everywhere in the world. The law of one price will make the price of all traded goods the same when expressed in the same currency. PPP (absolute or relative), however, is not about the price of individual goods, but about all goods. There are non-traded goods, whose prices, when expressed in the same currency, are not identical. The exchange rate will reflect the law of one price in trade goods, but it may not reflect relative prices of non-traded goods.

b) If absolute PPP does not hold, then the real exchange rate, $(P^{¥})(R)/P^{\$}$, will not be equal to 1.0. If, though, relative PPP holds, then the change in the exchange rate will reflect the difference in inflation rates, so the real exchange rate will not change. If the real exchange rate is 2.0, so that absolute PPP does not hold, then it will remain at 2.0 if relative PPP holds.

c) No, capital movements also affect exchange rates and capital movements are motivated by factors other than relative prices.

5. a) The monetary approach considers equilibrium in both the goods and monetary markets. If one is out of equilibrium, then the other market is affected. The elasticity approach focuses on the goods market, which is part of the monetary approach.

b) The asset approach considers simultaneous in the goods and asset markets. Money is one asset of many.

6. a) If price level increases at the same time and by the same proportionate amount as the change in the money supply, then according to PPP, the domestic exchange rate will depreciate simultaneously by that same amount. If the exchange rate is defined as R = $/fc, where fc is foreign currency, then R will increase (a depreciation of the dollar) at the same time as the money supply increases, as shown in the figure to the right.

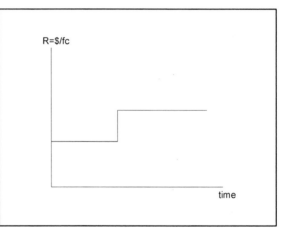

The interest rate will not be affected because an increase in the money supply by, say, 10%, and a simultaneous increase in the price level by 10% leaves the real money supply unchanged, so the interest rate will not change.

b) If the price level does not immediately react to the increase in the money supply, then the real money supply increases, which causes an initial decrease in the interest rate. By uncovered parity, this must mean, given foreign interest rates, that the foreign currency must be expected to depreciate. (It is assumed that i and i^{*} are initially equal.) If the foreign currency will appreciate in the long run, then the only way that foreign currency can be expected to depreciate now is if it overshoots its long-run value. The exchange rate will initially move above its long-

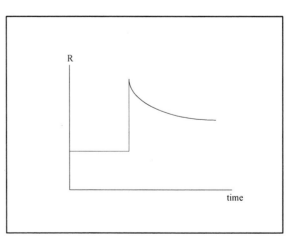

run value, and then slowly approach its long-run value as prices slowly increase. The time path of the exchange rate in this case is shown in the figure to the right.

Chapter 13: Automatic Adjustments with Flexible and Fixed Exchange Rates

Multiple Choice Questions

1. b
2. b
3. a
4. d
5. b
6. c
7. d
8. d
9. b
10. b

Problems and Discussion Questions

1. A depreciation of the dollar will increase the demand for U.S. exports and increase export prices, when expressed in the domestic currency. The same depreciation will decrease the supply of imports and increase import prices, when expressed in the domestic currency. These increased prices will feed directly into higher inflation rates. In addition, other prices in the domestic economy will increase as consumers substitute into domestic goods in response to high import prices and high export industry prices. (Export goods are also sold domestically.)

   If inflation increases in the domestic economy, this may produce another balance of payments deficit as buyers substitute into foreign goods, requiring further depreciation, which further increases inflation, etc. Depreciation in an inflationary economy will require macro policies that will reduce the rate of inflation.

2. a) Gold movements are motivated by exchange rates that differ from the underlying prices of gold between countries. For example if the United States agrees to peg gold at $50 per ounce, and the United Kingdom agrees to peg gold at £10 per ounce, then the implied exchange rate is $5/£1. If, on the foreign exchange market, the pound goes to, say, $5.50/£1, then pounds will not be purchased on the foreign exchange market. Those needing pounds that have dollars will buy gold in the United States for $50 and ship it to the United Kingdom where £5 can be purchased. Shipping gold at the maintained gold prices always insures that pounds can be had for $5 per pound.

b) Continuing the example in part a), if the pound is moving to $5.50/£1, then it is because there is an excess demand for pounds at $5.00/£1, or there is a US balance of payments deficit. As gold moves out of the U.S. into the United Kingdom, as explained in part a), then the money supply will fall in the U.S. (money is taken out of circulation by domestics to buy gold from the government). The decrease in the money supply will lower prices, which will restore U.S. competitiveness and correct the balance of payments deficit. In the meantime, the opposite will occur in the U.K. In the U.K. there will be a gold inflow, increasing U.K. prices and eliminating the U.K. surplus.

3. a) The U.S. demand for imports, with pound prices on the vertical axis, shifts vertically down by the same proportion as the depreciation. If the demand curve is vertical, then a vertical shift down produces no change. Consumers do not respond to a change in price caused by depreciation. The price of imports is unchanged and the quantity is unchanged, so the quantity demanded of foreign exchange is unaffected by a change in the exchange rate. This is shown in the accompanying figure by a vertical demand curve.

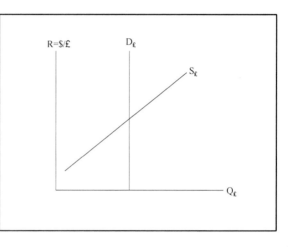

The depreciation of the dollar has the effect of shifting the supply of exports to the right, when pound prices are measured on the vertical axis. In this case the value of exports measured in pounds increases from 200 (50x4) to 240 (80x3). (See price and quantities in the question.) As the dollar cost of the pound, $/£, increases (depreciation of the dollar), the quantity of pounds supplied from the U.K. increases, so the supply of pounds is upward sloping, as shown in the accompanying figure.

With a vertical demand curve and an upward sloping supply curve, the foreign exchange market is stable. Stability means that excess demand will cause a change in the price (exchange rate) that eliminates itself, and excess supply will cause a change in the price that eliminates itself. (Verify in the accompanying figure that excess supply, which causes R=$/£ to decrease, will cause the excess supply to fall. Verify in the accompanying figure that excess demand, which causes R=$/£ to increase, will cause the excess demand to fall.)

b) The demand curve for imports shifts down due to the depreciation, and as can be seen in the figure for Question 3, part b), the price and quantity falls. Depreciation reduces the amount of pounds needed for imports, so the demand curve for foreign exchange is downward sloping.

The supply curve of exports shifts to the right, but the amount of pounds needed by the United Kingdom to buy exports is unchanged at 100. Price multiplied by quantity is identical at both intersections. This produces a vertical supply curve of foreign exchange.

A vertical supply of foreign exchange and a downward sloping demand curve for foreign exchange produces a stable foreign exchange market. As in part a), verify that the foreign exchange market is stable by showing that excess demand or supply will produce a change in price that eliminates that excess.

c) The demand for imports is vertical and so is unaffected by the depreciation. Because the value of imports is not affected by depreciation, the amount of pounds demanded for imports will not change. The demand curve for foreign exchange is vertical.

The demand for exports is vertical so the supply shift reduces the price of exports but leaves the quantity unaffected. Because the price is lower and quantity is unaffected, the United Kingdom needs to supply less foreign exchange as a result of depreciation. The supply curve for foreign exchange is *downward* sloping.

A vertical demand curve for foreign exchange and a downward sloping supply curve produce an unstable foreign exchange market. If the exchange rate, R=$/£, increases, then there will be excess demand, which causes a further increase in R, which causes greater excess demand, etc.

4. Case c) of Question 3 is consistent with the J-curve phenomenon. A depreciation of the dollar will cause further excess demand for foreign exchange, which is a larger balance of payments deficit. Notice that this case is one in which the price elasticity of demand for both imports and exports is zero. In the short run, price elasticities do tend to be low. The J-curve phenomenon exists because elasticities are low, but then increase (in absolute value) as time passes. In time, the demand curves will be downward sloping and the depreciation will improve a balance of payments deficit.

5. a) Set Y=C+I+X-M. Solving for Y, Y=1500.

b) X-M=300-(50+.25Y)=300-(50+375)= -25.

c) New Y=1700.

d) X-M=300-(50+.25Y)=300-(50+425)= +25.
The increase in exports of 100 causes output/income to increase by a multiple, which generates new imports. The increase in exports of 100 causes imports to increase so the trade balance does not increase by the increases in exports.

6. a) Foreign recession will reduce foreign imports, which are Kenya's exports, so Kenya's trade balance will become negative. The reduction in exports will also reduce Kenya's income level. The lower income level will provide some adjustment to trade deficit produced by the decreased exports because at lower levels of income, imports will be lower. The deficit caused by the reduction in exports (partially offset by the reduced imports) will put downward pressure on Kenya's exchange rate. To defend the exchange rate, the monetary authorities of Kenya must buy their own currency with foreign exchange reserves. This will reduce Kenya's money supply, which will have the effect of further contracting Kenya's output, and will reduce Kenya's price levels. The money supply will contract as long as there is a deficit putting pressure on the exchange rate, so this process will continue until the lower income and lower prices restore trade balance. In addition, the lower money supply will raise interest rates and attract capital to Kenya, providing private financing for the trade deficit. At the new equilibrium, there may still be a trade deficit financed by the capital inflows. It's not clear what happens to import-competing

sectors. The reduced income will mean less domestic activity, but the lower price level will reduce imports, shifting some demand to import-competing sectors.

b) The adjustment requires a reduction in domestic income, directly from the reduced exports, and indirectly from the lower money supply. Kenya may resist letting its economy move into recession as a result of automatic adjustments to a trade deficit.

Chapter 14: Adjustment Policies

Multiple Choice Questions

1. c
2. c
3. b
4. d
5. c
6. b
7. a
8. b
9. b
10. c

Problems and Discussion Questions

1. With fixed exchange rates, money is not effective internally, but can affect the external balance. This means fiscal policy should be directed towards internal balance.

a) Contractionary monetary and fiscal policy.

b) Contractionary monetary policy and expansionary fiscal policy.

c) Expansionary monetary policy and contractionary fiscal policy.

d) Expansionary monetary and fiscal policy.

2. a) Although contractionary fiscal policy will reduce imports by reducing income, capital movements are much larger than changes in imports. Contractionary fiscal policy will reduce interest rates and produce a capital outflow. The capital outflow will threaten to depreciate the dollar so the monetary authorities will buy the dollar with reserves which reduces the money supply.

b) Both the contractionary fiscal policy and the resulting decrease in the money supply will reduce output and income.

3. a) An expansionary money supply will lower interest rates and produce a capital outflow. Monetary authorities will have to defend the exchange rate by buying the dollar, reducing the money supply. The net effect will be no change in the money supply.

b) With no change in the money supply, output and income will be unaffected.

4. Fiscal policy is ineffective with floating exchange rates, so monetary policy should be used in both cases.

a) Expansionary monetary policy.

b) Contractionary monetary policy.

5. a) The withdrawal of funds will threaten to depreciate the exchange rate. The monetary authorities will support the exchange rate by buying the currency, which reduces the money supply.

b) The reduction in the money supply will reduce output and income.

6. a) The demand for the nation's exports will increase as foreign nations' incomes increase. The increased demand for exports will increase the demand for the nation's currency. (In addition, the increased demand in the nation will mean an increased demand for money, which will increase interest rates. The higher interest rates will attract capital and demand for the nation's currency.) To maintain the fixed exchange rate, the nation will satisfy the new demand by supplying new money.

b) The increased demand for exports plus the increased money supply will increase output and income.

7. a) A reduction in the money supply will lead to lower interest rates and capital outflow. The capital outflow will depreciate the exchange rate, stimulating net exports. Net exports are part of aggregate demand so output and income will also increase. (Note that interest rates cannot fall if capital if very mobile, for capital will move to equate interest rates. Monetary policy with capital mobility does not work through investment as in a closed economy, but through its effect on the exchange rate and net exports.)

b) Contractionary fiscal policy, by lowering the demand for funds, lowers the interest rate, producing capital outflow and depreciation of the dollar. The depreciation of the dollar will stimulate net exports, which offsets the contractionary fiscal policy. Fiscal policy is ineffective with fixed exchange rates and high capital mobility.

Chapter 15: Flexible versus Fixed Exchange Rates, European Monetary Systems, and Macroeconomic Policy Coordination

Multiple Choice Questions

1. d
2. a
3. a
4. d
5. d
6. d
7. b
8. b
9. c
10. a

Problems and Discussion Questions

1. a) A flexible exchange-rate system is considered more efficient because the floating rate continuously maintains balance of payments equilibrium. In a fixed exchange rate system, external payments imbalances are transmitted to changes in the money supply, and, in turn, to domestic prices and incomes. It is more efficient for one price to change-the exchange rate-than for all domestic prices to change.

b) The EU has adopted one currency -the Euro- in order to reduce the cost exchange rate uncertainty associated with flexible rates, and in order to reduce the clerical costs of exchanging money.

2. a) If you favor a fixed exchange rate system, you might view speculation as destabilizing under flexible exchange rates and stabilizing under fixed exchange rate systems. If governments establish a *credible* fixed rate, then private participants will not bet against the ability of governments to maintain the exchange rate. If the exchange rate reaches the limit of its band, then private speculators will bet that it will return to its central value, and their actions will cause it to move towards the central value.

b) If you favor a flexible exchange rate system, then you would view speculation as stabilizing under flexible rates. You would argue that speculators would not, on average, be wrong about the movement of exchange rates. If speculators are correct, then they will buy low and sell high, chopping off the peaks and valleys of exchange rate movements.

    A proponent of floating rates would argue that speculation is destabilizing under fixed rates. Fixed rates change very infrequently, and when it is clear that a change should be made, it's public news. Speculators acting on the public news will have a sure bet, and actually be a cause of a change in the exchange rate.

3. As an example, suppose the internal disturbance is a decrease in domestic income. With fixed exchange rates, a decrease in domestic income will decrease imports. The reduction in imports reduces the demand for foreign currency, threatening to appreciate the domestic currency. Monetary authorities will respond by selling domestic currency, which reduces the money supply, the effects of which will offset the initial decrease in domestic income.

With floating rates, the decrease in imports due to domestic contraction will cause the domestic currency to appreciate. The appreciation of the domestic currency will cause fewer exports and more imports, thus adding to the contraction.

With internal disturbances, a nation would prefer a fixed exchange rate system because the resulting monetary change will offset the internal disturbance. With a floating–rate system, the internal disturbance will amplify the internal disturbance.

4. The anchor argument is that a fixed exchange rate will help curb inflationary pressures. If the exchange rate is fixed relative to a major trading partner with a low rate of inflation, then any excessive domestic inflation will cause a balance of payments deficit. The deficit will threaten to weaken the domestic currency, which will lead to purchases of the domestic currency by the domestic monetary authorities. Purchases of the domestic currency will decrease the domestic supply of money and reduce inflationary pressures. The strength of the anchor argument lies in the commitment to the fixed exchange rate. A question that arises is why would governments be more committed to a fixed exchange rate than to a lower rate of inflation directly? If governments were committed to a lower rate of inflation directly, then inflation could be controlled directly by controlling the money supply.

5. a) If a nation chooses an inflation rate higher than its trading partners, then a fixed exchange rate system would be inappropriate. Higher relative inflation would continuously threaten to depreciate the domestic currency as both domestic and foreign buyers continually substitute into the goods of the nation with lower inflation. The exchange rate system would not necessarily have to be a freely floating one, but would have to be constructed such that continual currency devaluations could be easily and effectively made.

b) A fixed exchange rate system. If a government commits to a fixed exchange rate, then the currency pressures of high domestic inflation would produce monetary contraction and a lower inflation rate. This is the anchor argument. See Question 4.

6. First, the United States has one central bank. Consequently, the United States has one underlying common rate of inflation, although some regions' inflation rates may differ slightly. In Latin America, each nation has a central bank and each nation has a different inflation rate. Before a common currency could be considered for Latin America, inflation rates would have to converge, after which a common central bank could be established.

Next, labor mobility is much higher in the United States. It is much easier to relocate from, say, Ohio to Virginia than it is to relocate from the mountains of Peru to Ecuador. A common currency area eliminates the exchange rate as an adjustment mechanism. A non–competitive nation in Latin America will find its currency depreciating, leading to a stimulation of exports and a contraction of imports. In the United States, a non-competitive region adjusts, in part, by a movement of labor to competitive regions.

Finally, the United States has a central fiscal agent that has the power to redistribute income from wealthy regions to poor regions. Latin America has many national governments that do not have the power to tax one nation in order to redistribute to other nations.

7. In a flexible exchange–rate system, exchange rate uncertainty is borne by the private participants in the foreign exchange market. Importers, exporters, and holders of foreign assets confront exchange-risk directly and must decide whether to bet on exchange-rate changes or hedge foreign exchange risk by using forward and options contracts.

In a fixed exchange-rate system, the government agrees to maintain the exchange rate by appropriate exchange rate intervention. The cost of holding reserves and the cost of administrative expenses and staff is borne by taxpayers. The cost of events that would cause changes in the exchange rate is spread over all taxpayers.

Chapter 16: The International Monetary System: Past, Present, and Future

Multiple Choice Questions

1. d
2. c
3. b
4. c
5. a
6. b
7. a
8. c
9. c
10. b

Problems and Discussion Questions

1. a) Under the gold standard, each participating nation agreed to stand ready to buy and sell gold at an agreed price. In doing, so they fixed the price of gold by satisfying all private excess demands and supplies. The fixed price of gold in each nation also implied a fixed price of currencies.

b) Under the Bretton Woods system, the United States agreed to fix the price of gold in dollars. All other participating nations agreed to fix the price of their currency relative to the dollar, with a band of 1% on either side of the agreed upon par value.

2. a) In order for world trade to expand, which would bring larger deficits and surpluses, it was necessary for the level of reserves to increase steadily. Because dollars were the principal reserve currency, this meant that the world relied upon a steady supply of dollars to the world. In order for the supply of dollars to increase, the United States had to run continual current account deficits. These continual deficits, though, would threaten the confidence in the dollars. The continually increasing supply of dollars led holders of dollars to believe, rightly, that the value of the dollar would have to fall. It was impossible to continue to hold and use a reserve currency whose value everyone knew would fall.

b) The SDR is international money created by the IMF. It is created through accounting entries that each country agrees to accept in exchange for its own currency. The purpose of the SDR was to increase the level of reserves in the world (increase liquidity) without increasing the number of dollars in circulation.

3. a) For a country facing continual balance of payments deficits, the exchange rate would reach the bottom of the band against the dollar, after which the country would buy its own currency with dollars. This would reduce the country's money supply, causing a reduction in domestic prices and income. Lower prices would stimulate exports and contract imports, and lower income would contract imports, thus correcting the balance of payments deficit.

b) Because the automatic adjustment meant lower domestic incomes for deficit countries, the automatic changes in the money supply were often offset through expansionary open market operations. The contractionary effect of the automatic adjustment could also be offset by expansionary fiscal policies.

c) If countries resisted the automatic changes in the money supply, then adjustment to deficits would not occur. Without adjustment, deficits continue and so must be financed with reserves. In time, reserves run out and the currency must devalue. Periods prior to devaluation were rather obvious because of the effect on reserves, so destabilizing speculation occurred, hastening the need for devaluation.

4. a) The experience with beggar-thy-neighbor policies and competitive devaluations between the wars convinced nations that trade and growth would best be promoted by a fixed exchange rate system.

b) The basic role of the IMF was to provide an orderly financing and adjustment of international payments imbalances with fixed exchange rates. It did this by providing lending to deficit nations to finance imbalances, as well as by providing technical and legal assistance.

5. Destabilizing speculation was a major problem of the Bretton Woods system primarily because the provision for changes in the agreed–upon par values were not well specified. In practice, exchange rates were changed infrequently, and only when it became obvious to the world that currency devaluation was long overdue. This meant that speculators could take rather

safe bets in foreign exchange markets. If it became apparent that the pound would have to devalue, then speculators would sell the pound, making their expectations realized.

6. a) The current international monetary system is made up of many types of exchange rate systems. Some small countries fix their currency to that of a major trading partner, while some other small countries fix to a basket of currencies, like the SDR. Many large countries have relatively flexible exchange rates, but do intervene on a regular basis to try to smooth short-term fluctuations without resisting long-term changes in the exchange rate. Notably, the EU has adopted the Euro as its single currency. In general, however, exchange rates are more flexible than they were under the Bretton Woods system.

b) The major problems of the currency international monetary system include excessive volatility of exchange rates and periodic financial crises in emerging market economies due to freer movement of capital across international borders.

Breinigsville, PA USA
23 July 2010
242272BV00002B/2/P